MODELLING MILITARY VEHICLES

Bill Evans

Contributor
David Parker

ROBERT HALE · LONDON

Copyright © Bill Evans and David Parker 1990
First published in Great Britain 1990

Robert Hale Limited
Clerkenwell House
Clerkenwell Green
London EC1R 0HT

British Library Cataloguing in Publication Data

Evans, Bill
  Modelling military vehicles.
  1. Model military vehicles. Construction
  I. Title   II. Parker, David
  623.74′7′0228

  ISBN 0–7090–4021–0

Set in Century Schoolbook by
Derek Doyle & Associates, Mold, Clwyd.
Printed and bound in Great Britain by
Butler & Tanner Ltd., Frome, Somerset.

MODELLING MILITARY VEHICLES

Contents

Illustrations

Acknowledgements

Many people have helped me during the preparation of this book. David Parker's contribution naturally made a vast difference to the finished product – during hours of discussion we thrashed out many matters. Gordon MacLaughlin provided a massive amount of reference material, frequently at very short notice. Andy Hodgson knew all about the availability of kits, including many of the more exotic items, and seemed to know about the release of new items before the manufacturers did! I was able to plan one of the sections of the book thanks to the information he provided. Alan Ranger of Arba Models and Frank Campy of the Kit Box Model Shop sought out and obtained many of the less usual items used. Derek Hansen of Accurate Armour and Gordon Brown of Cromwell Models showed me how the smaller manufacturers managed to make the best models you can lay your hands on: that experience was a real eye-opener. Many thanks are also due to Erik Johansen and Paul Williams, who allowed me to use photographs of their models to illustrate certain points made in the book. Both are members of the Tyneside branch of the International Plastic Modellers Society. Finally, thanks are due to the chairman of this group, Rob Sullivan, who showed me what a pleasure it could be to belong to a well-run society.

B.E.

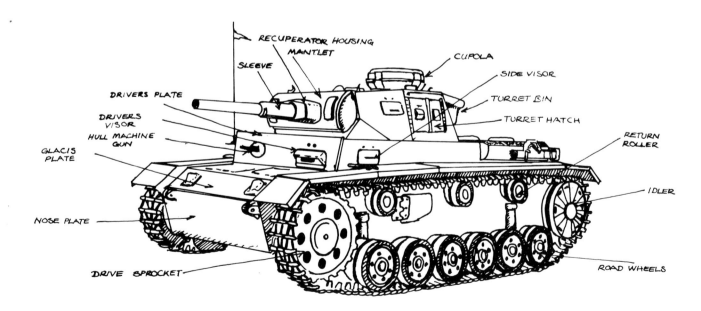

Introduction

The age-old problems in warfare are: how best to close with the enemy; how best to strike him down; and how to remain immune to his efforts to do the same to you. Quite obviously the qualities needed are a combination of mobility, striking-power and protection.

By the mid seventeenth century it was evident that striking-power, in the form of artillery and muskets, was capable of defeating any armour that could be worn or carried by a man even when he was mounted upon a horse. Protection could be given by fortifications, but as these constructions were immobile they could be isolated by otherwise victorious forces and pounded into submission.

This state of affairs pertained well into the present century. The major advances made were the greatly increased destructiveness of the weapons themselves and the ability of industrialized societies to train, equip and deliver mass armies to the battlefield via the railway systems. When World War I began the first lesson learned was that two inventions of the late nineteenth century – the breech-loading 'rapid-fire' field gun and the machine gun – dominated the battlefield and made movement virtually impossible. The only way that infantry could survive was by digging into the ground: trench warfare began. The war rapidly began to resemble a vast siege, and the problem of how to close with the enemy dominated military thought. Armour protection was the key to the success of battleships, which dominated naval operations, and the idea of a 'land battleship' was conceived. Powered by another invention of the late nineteenth century, the internal combustion engine, and travelling on endless tracks, an armoured vehicle could close with the enemy and destroy him with the direct fire weapons that they carried. The first tanks were used by the British Army in 1916, and although the impact they had on operations was minimal, they at least demonstrated the massive potential of these fearsome machines. The rather curious title of 'tanks' was bestowed upon these machines since, during development, they were referred to as water tanks in order to disguise their true purpose from the enemy. As these vehicles progressed technologically it became obvious that they would become an integral part of the military machine. Indeed had the war continued past 1918 the British Army would have attacked the enemy with a largely mechanized force.

During the interwar period the German Army took to heart the lessons of the previous conflict and made equipping themselves with armoured vehicles a high priority. Not only did they build 'classic' tanks, by this time fully shielded vehicles with the main armament mounted in a revolving turret and most of the armoured protection at the front, they also mounted artillery upon tracked, armoured chassis and provided armoured half-tracked vehicles so that some infantry could operate alongside their tanks. They also built large numbers of armoured cars, really the very first type of armoured fighting vehicle. Concentrated into the famous Panzer divisions these vehicles formed the spearhead of the German Army and were largely responsible for its sweeping successes during the initial stages of the Second World War. Gradually, the Allies gained the upper hand, but one factor emerged: armoured vehicles dominated the battlefield and would be indispensable in future operations.

Although the impending demise of the tank has been frequently forecast during the sixties and seventies, recent events have tended, if anything, to emphasize its importance. Many military writers have tried to classify the tank as a development of an older weapon, for example armoured cavalry or mobile artillery, but whilst there is some credibility in their views, the tank remains a unique weapon in land warfare; it has had as much effect upon military procedure as the submarine or the aircraft.

In present-day armies all arms of service are protected by armour and given mobility by endless tracks or multi-wheeled drive. Main battle tanks (MBTs) can travel at speeds of up to 50 mph, are protected, in their most vulnerable areas, by armour thicker than that carried by World War II battleships and are equipped with a gun which is capable of piercing this same amount of armour. Infantry are transported in armoured personnel carriers (APCs) or the fashionable mechanized infantry combat vehicles (MICVs), a vehicle type which no one seems quite sure how to use. Most artillery is tracked and armoured, as are command posts, signals vehicles, recovery vehicles, engineer vehicles, supply carriers and so on.

The first model tanks that appeared were probably made from wood and card by schoolboys, but the first commercial items that I know of were Staffordshire pottery efforts, finished in a white glaze with gold trimming, and sold to raise money for a 'patriotic fund' in 1916. I have also seen some very fine cast-bronze pieces but these seem to have been made for presentation purposes only.

During the twenties die-cast models began to appear, as did some cut-out models printed, in colour, on thin card.

The hobby really began to take off during the 1950s, when the first injection-moulded plastic kits appeared in the United States. The first ones that I recall were the 1/32nd-scale series of the then current American equipment produced by Renwall. They were very fine models indeed, being quite accurate, incorporating fine detail and featuring, where appropriate, flexible vinyl tracks. This last feature was a bit of a 'play' feature as it allowed the running gear to move, though it was also something of a fiction since the running gear never did stand up to much exercise and the scale appearance was somewhat compromised by it. Nevertheless, this feature of flexible plastic tracks has remained with us to this day. The next range of models which appeared was in 1/48th scale and, again, good quality. In the early sixties the British firm of Airfix brought out a range of models in 1/76th scale and the hobby really began to take off. They were first-class models in their day and launched many an enthusiast into the hobby. They were available at pocket-money prices and this made them very accessible to younger modellers, as well as the fact that they were very easy to construct. At the same time several hobby magazines began to appear, reference material became readily available and clubs such as the Miniature Armoured Fighting Vehicles Association and the International Plastic Modellers Society were formed to cater for those with a deeper interest in the pastime.

The seventies saw a massive expansion in the hobby with the introduction of 1/35th scale and several specialist publications. It was a boom time for the hobby and it seemed that every boy from about the age of eight upwards was making plastic kits. Enthusiasts were converting kits to different variants and scratch building their own models, and the standard of kits became really excellent. But, like all booms, it eventually ground to a halt, owing to changes of fashion, and it began to contract and find its true level.

The 1980s saw the introduction of specialist kits usually made by enthusiasts for enthusiasts. These small manufacturers have generally produced kits of remarkable quality and have contributed greatly to the present revival of interest in the hobby. Besides producing kits of the less commercial subjects demanded by the keen hobbyist, they also manufacture a range of conversion kits and accessories. Usually (for no very good reason) known as the cottage industry, these small concerns have a high profile and their success seems to have made the bigger concerns take notice and re-release kits and even offer new items.

The hobbyist, in the words of one ex-prime minister, 'has never had it so good'. Kits covering the majority of subjects and in most scales are available, as are a multitude of figures and accessories. Moreover, the mass of reference material means that there is no longer the necessity to become involved in complex research.

Unfortunately the less experienced modeller may find that there is simply too much to take in once he becomes involved in the hobby: too many kits to choose from; too much reference material; and too many accessories. It is hoped this book will help the newer modeller come to terms with this situation. It assumes that you can assemble a kit and have a deep commitment to the hobby, and it goes on from there. Kits are explored in some depth, including some of the more exotic items available. Making a good one better and making a poor one come up to scratch are then covered, as is painting, weathering, crew figures and presentation. After this, we get our teeth into 'real' modelling as opposed to kit assembly. The art of kit conversion is tackled and then the ultimate challenge that the hobby has to offer – that of building a model from scratch – is explored. All these projects are fully illustrated with practical examples and graded for the degree of experience needed to complete them in a competent manner.

Price is an important factor in any hobby. However, even modest inflation makes any attempt to indicate a cost something of a nonsense. Bearing this in mind, I have adopted a rough and ready indication of the *relative* prices of the more exotic models. Simply find the price of a plastic model about the same size and multiply it by the factor indicated; for example, the Gunze Sangyo 'hi tech' Pz III costs about six times the price of its Tamiya equivalent.

Enjoy your modelling!

Bill Evans
May 1990

This 1/76th-scale resin kit from Cromwell is probably the best model of the famous Panther yet released. Cromwell also make an equally good early variant which is vastly superior to the early 1/35th-scale Japanese offerings, even though it's less than half the size.

1 Kits

One thing that almost all currently available kits have in common is that they are of excellent quality. Oddly enough, kits of less well-known vehicles are usually better as regards accuracy and fineness of detail than those of the more famous vehicles. The reason for this is quite clear. When a manufacturer introduces a range of military vehicles, the early ones must sell well enough to establish the range; everything improves with practice and so the later models show a distinct improvement over the earlier efforts. At the same time, models of the more famous tanks always sell very well indeed and, if something is still going well, why alter it? It must be stressed that the difference in quality is merely comparative: even the early kits are first-rate models. Nevertheless, a supporting industry has grown round the early releases, especially in the larger scales, and they are now providing replacement parts for those not up to current standards.

Scales

Although vehicles are available in a range of scales from 1/300th scale models intended for wargames to 1/15th scale monsters which may be fitted with remote control, most modellers would accept that there are only two real scales: 1/76th and 1/35th. There really should be three! 1/76th is the same scale as 0.0 railways. It was popularized by the British firm Airfix, whose super range of models started off most of the current 'veteran' modellers. For quite a long while this was *the* scale for modellers who were primarily interested in armoured vehicles. The reasons for the appeal of this small scale were the small size of the models which allowed a large collection to be displayed, the 'pocket money' prices and, most important of all in my opinion, the very high quality of the models themselves – models in this scale can hold a surprising amount of detail. Larger scales were mainly the preserve of the 54 mm model soldier collector who perhaps wanted some armoured fighting vehicles (AFVs) to set off a collection of modern figures. 54 mm is, in effect, 1/32nd scale which is a lovely, logical scale to work in at ⅜ inch to the foot. Some vehicles were made in this scale and there was a small but dedicated band of scratch builders who showed just what could be achieved in this larger scale.

Then, rather more than twenty years ago, 1/35th scale appeared. Its origin was Japan, a country with no model soldier tradition as there is in Europe or the USA. It would seem that the scale was chosen in a rather arbitrary fashion firstly because it was a convenient size, secondly because it was suitable for motorization and finally because it was a size which would package well. The first models were dreadful. They could be described at best as tank-shaped, self-assembly toys. Detail was shaky to say the least and any 'scalishness' (i.e. the accuracy of the relationship between models and real thing) which the models accidentally possessed was hopelessly compromised by the need to make them mobile. This made for very crude rubber-band tracks and very peculiar running gear.

The Tamiya Panther being taken up to the same standards and being converted to the same late pattern. The Tamiya turret is far too big and a new one has been fabricated. For all this, the early Tamiya item makes up to a handome-looking model.

The tiny electric motors that were provided were not good either. They were generally very unreliable and usually gave the model a radius of action about the length of an average living room along which they would lurch in the fashion of a rather erratic clockwork mouse before they stopped, whereupon the motor could never again be coaxed into action.

Of course everyone involved in the hobby despised these funny, wrong-sized items and confidently expected them to go away. After all, 1/32nd was the 'proper' larger scale. 1/35th didn't go away, instead it improved to an amazing extent and when feedback suggested

that modellers were unhappy with the discrepancy in scales between their 54 mm soldiers and the new scale, 1/35th scale model soldiers were introduced at very competitive prices. The late counter attack by British and American firms was shrugged off and the 1/32nd scale items, some of which were outstandingly good, are no longer with us. The models illustrating this book are all to a scale of 1/35th, which is perfect for illustrating the techniques described.

I made the rather strange remark earlier that whilst there were two established scales, there should have been three. In fact for a while there were three scales, the one missing today being 1/48th scale which is perhaps the most logical of all. It exactly matched aircraft in that scale, was capable of appearing as 'scalish' as 1/35th scale, yet was easily stored so that a collection took up little space. Always more popular in America than Europe, 1/48th scale never really caught on as it should have done, especially as the models available in the scale were of such a very high standard. I gather there are plans afoot to reintroduce this lovely range of models. I hope that this time the scale will succeed in establishing itself – it deserves to.

Reference material

Most of us get involved in vehicle modelling because of an interest in things military. We therefore have a clear idea of the subject matter upon which our modelling will be based. If your interest in the hobby was, for example, sparked off by reading several accounts of the War in the Desert (1940/43) then you will have a good idea of the vehicles involved and their appearance. From there it is simply a question of going to the local model shop and seeing what is available. This seems a logical step but, as always in life, things are never quite that straightforward. Say, for example, that you want to model the Panzer IV. There are at least two types available in each scale, an early model and a late type. Some vehicles are not available at all from 'normal' sources. The Panzer III is a late pattern and not really representative of the vehicles which fought in the early part of the conflict and the same appears to be the case with the Crusader. Obviously some more specific knowledge of the subject is called for.

The ideal basis for a collection of reference material is one of the military hobby magazines. In addition to the sometimes excellent articles there are all sorts of advertisements and reviews showing just what is available. From then on it is simply a matter of getting some general primers and hunting out publications upon specific areas. Another good idea is to go to a local, small, independent retailer.

The people who own these shops usually regard them as a vocation; they live and breathe models and are extremely knowledgeable on the subject. In their shops you will find all sorts of wonderful objects which would be 'uneconomic' for the high-street retailers. If it is available, they will know of it and be able to get it. They can also put you in contact with the local modelling club or society, at whose meetings you will meet other keen modellers. Many of the 'veterans' will have amassed a vast amount of knowledge which they will be only too willing to share. As your interest in the hobby grows so will your source material; it's an inevitable process.

Tools

You need really very few tools to begin with. This simple statement frequently comes as rather a shock to newer modellers as it is assumed that modelling ability is in direct proportion to the amount of equipment possessed! In fact there is a tendency towards 'equipmentitis' within the hobby. Lack of specialized and frequently expensive tools is often given as a reason for lack of finished models. Quite simply, it's not so much what you have got, it's the way that you use it.

The most important modelmaking tool that you can buy is the craft knife. A knife is a wonderful tool. Obviously you can cut and carve with it but you can also scrape, smooth, hold parts in position, adjust parts, remove mould marks, score, model and drill etc. It is best to get a good one such as the Exacto which is made in the USA but is available everywhere. The versatility of the knife can be enhanced by the type of blade fitted. A short-pointed blade is best for general cutting and removing parts from the sprue whilst a long-pointed one is ideal for 'drilling' and

Early reference material now no longer available; if you spot this sort of stuff second hand in a specialist book/model shop or at a club 'swap meet', snap it up.

Go to a small independent model shop. These all specialize to some extent and the owners tend to be well informed.

holding small parts against the bulk of the model until they can be secured with a wash of cement. Other types of blades are useful in certain situations; for example, a curved blade is excellent for carving and some modellers say that these are by far the best for removing kit parts from the sprue. Another very useful type which is frequently disregarded is the chisel blade. This can be exceptionally useful for 'chopping' and removing cement and mould marks. Of course you can (eventually) manage to do all this with one blade, but having the correct ones does make life easier! As always, there are individual preferences; for example, I prefer the slightly heavier gauge of knife; fortunately one is available in the same range as the Exacto. However, as I do a lot of converting and scratch building, a heavier knife and blade is useful for battering through substantial thicknesses of plastic. Some modellers prefer a lighter knife, such as a scalpel, but these are relatively delicate instruments and are perhaps more suited to the very experienced modelmaker.

The other essential tools are sandpaper and files. Sandpaper in this case is a general term for all abrasive papers; you will need a couple of sheets in medium/fine and fine. Pieces of sandpaper glued to strips or half formed around dowelling or cocktail sticks make very precise tools but for real precision a selection of Swiss files is best – if only there were some way of preventing them from clogging!

One tool with which every modeller should equip himself with is a steel rule. You are going to need a rule if you intend to advance beyond the very simple assembly of kits, so buy a good one.

These tools are the essential ones. There are others, however, which it is particularly useful to have. They do not cost anything to run, so they can be classed as a useful investment.

They are a razor saw, a 'junior' hacksaw, (buy one of these in preference to a razor saw) and an electric modeller's drill; a soldering iron, one of the electric variety, also has its uses. All these tools are genuinely helpful and other, more specialized, types will be dealt with as appropriate. Nevertheless, there are many tools on the market which seem to provide solutions to problems which do not exist. It is best to learn to use the few tools which form the basis of all modelling outfits.

A heavy 'Lino' knife is useful for cutting through major kit parts, such as suspension arms or turrets.

A good heavy general-purpose knife. The blade is good for cutting or chopping.

A lighter knife. This type of blade is suitable for 'drilling', fine cutting and scraping.

A cheap, general-purpose craft knife. The curved blade is very good for removing parts from the sprue.

Materials

If we assume that the basic materials are model kits, then the secondary materials are adhesives and fillers whilst the tertiary ones are constructional and detailing items.

Models are stuck together with adhesives. The best one for plastics is liquid cement, a material which has almost completely taken over from tube cement as far as the serious modeller is concerned. Most non-plastic kits are best assembled with either one of the 'superglues' or a material that these relative newcomers have by no means made obsolete, epoxy resin. Needless to say, contact adhesive and PVA-type adhesives are also very useful. Indeed, there are times when they are the only materials that will do the job.

A filler is also essential – and there are two types. One kind is simply applied to small gaps or blemishes directly from the tube, allowed to dry and sanded smooth. Greenstuff is the best

of this type. The second kind is a two-part epoxy filler, which, though less convenient to use, can be modelled and formed (the figure in the tank on the jacket, for example, was modelled from this material). Milliput is the best for this – and comes in a pack as opposed to a tube. I now find both sorts indispensable.

If additions need to be made to basic kits then they must be built up from scratch or bought in the form of an accessory kit. If you intend to do it yourself then it is best to get acquainted with that staple material of the advanced modeller, sheet polystyrene, better known as plastic card/sheet and from now on referred to simply as 'sheet'. It is wonderful stuff and has, in my opinion, revolutionized the hobby. It is light, rigid and comes in a practical variety of thicknesses. It can easily be bonded both to itself and plastic kit parts and may be sanded, filed, drilled, carved, laminated, heat-formed, scored and cold-worked. These methods of working the material are, of course,

Masses of accessories are available from the smaller manufacturers, and can be seen at the specialist model shops.

in addition to the obvious one of simply cutting it to shape and building structures from it.

Another very useful material, sadly a 'low-tech' one currently out of fashion, is balsa wood. It is the best thing there is for carving bulky items such as cast turrets etc. The best way to buy this material is in sheet form, then laminations may be made to any desired thickness.

The cottage industry now supporting the hobby produces an amazing array of pieces. These range from pre-cut strips of sheet, plastic rod and tube to fitting kits in etched brass, superb machine guns, tracks and crew figures. The quality of some of these items has to be seen to be believed but in our opinion some of the solutions offered seem a little extreme.

The best place to see all of these materials and accessories is the small, specialist shop. Here you can examine them and often the owner or users will comment on their usefulness.

I think the best initial approach to adopt is the 'low-tech' one: equip yourself with sheet, wood, strip and rod, filler and various adhesives. Start from this basic outfit and then, as your involvement in the hobby grows, see if there is a need for the more exotic offerings.

Is there anything else?

Quite a lot actually. The first thing to discuss briefly is general modelling practice. You need somewhere to work. Most modellers start off working in a corner of the bedroom where space is restricted to say the least. One of the first lessons most veteran modelmakers thus learn is the importance of being ordered and tidy! Keep all your tools in one box and materials in another. Make only one model at a time and work upon it until it is at least assembled; if one has several projects going at once confusion sets in very quickly. Work from the kit box, return major assemblies to it, but keep small sub-assemblies in a small box and small parts, cut from the sprues, in another. A modelling board is virtually mandatory – it saves carving up the dressing table. A plastic-coated cutting board is the best thing to use as a modelling board. The plastic-coated type is best as it is firstly, very resistant to cutting, and secondly it does not warp, which is very useful when one progresses to scratch building.

At the end of each modelling session everything should be tidied away. Boxes and bottles should be capped, tools put away, scraps collected and dumped and the unexpended portions of materials cleaned up and put in their resting places. Get into a routine and never leave your working area in a mess; things always get lost. It is a good idea to have the top of a large kit box somewhere handy; this allows you to keep together bits recently assembled and in need of further drying out easily found and relatively safe. Such wholesome tidiness is not only pleasant for general working conditions but it is highly practical; you know where everything is and all small parts are together. Any experienced modeller will tell you that any small parts left out, and unattended, will probably vanish.

Commercial kits

As I remarked during the introduction, kits of military vehicles are nearly always excellent. Even the early models were very good and had been properly planned. The later 'third generation' ones are quite outstanding. Having said this, there is not a kit built model which cannot be improved, although some come close to perfection.

THE ITALERI PANZER I

This tiny model is quite superb and is at the peak of standard kit development. If fits together very well and is extremely accurate. The kit instructions are acceptable and no difficulty should be experienced during its construction. In fact the model gives the impression of having been designed by people who considered their allotted task a vocation rather than a tedious job.

Working method
Of course the basic construction of the real vehicle, itself very simple, makes for an uncomplicated model which, in turn, helps make the kit an easy one to construct. As it is obviously so simple there is always the danger, if that is not too strong a term, of the model simply being thrown together. As always, cut the parts carefully off the sprue, leave a slight stub of sprue on the part, then trim it off and scrape any mould marks off with the knife. Build up the model gradually, not removing parts until they are needed. It is a good idea to try to use the minimal amount of cement when fixing the model together; on this model the parts seem to snap together and great strong joints are not at all essential.

IMPROVING THE MODEL
All kits can be improved, and with this model one may improve upon the limitations of the plastic injection-moulding process. There are dimples in the centre of the boss on the drive sprockets. These should be filled in with a spot of filler applied with a toothpick or sharpened matchstick. It seems that nothing is quite as easy as it should be and in this instance the filler, which needs smoothing, is right in the middle of, and very close to, some delicate and essential detail. To get at this area it is necessary to make a tool. This consists of a

scrap of abrasive paper glued to a piece of rod then trimmed round. It can then be held against the filler and twisted between thumb and forefinger until the filler is smooth. Doubtless somewhere there is an expensive tool which, when fitted to an expensive drill, will do exactly the same job. However it is frequently possible to make up an inexpensive tool for a specialized job.

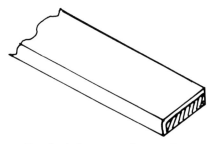

File away the shaded area as shown, at an angle, to give the impression of thin trackguards.

As the front portions of the trackguards were usually removed in service the thickness of this part is very apparent and looks far too thick and clumsy. It needs thinning and the ideal tool to do this is a flat Swiss file. As it is impractical to do this along the whole length of the part it is only necessary to thin the front portion which gives the correct effect. Figure 7 shows how this is done.

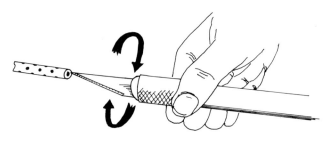

To 'drill out' gun barrels etc., insert the tip of a fine-pointed knife and twist as shown.

The Italeri Panzer I, showing the new exhaust cover, smoke-candle discharger, radio rod and induced track sag. Light, dry brushing highlights the vehicle's shape and texture.

Another improvement is to drill out the ends of the machine guns. This is quite easy to do; all it needs is a steady hand and a degree of confidence. You don't even need to invest in a drill as the craft knife serves perfectly well. Use a long-pointed blade, hold it lightly against the gun end and *gently* twist. It works very well indeed.

The radio rod is best cut away and replaced with one made from either thin rod or stretched sprue. One of the first tricks of the trade that most modellers learn is how to stretch sprue. It is simply a matter of holding a piece of kit sprue over a small flame, such as that given by a candle, and gently rotating it. When the sprue begins to smoke, blacken and droop, it is removed from the flame and then

stretched. The heated area stretches and thins to a fine filament which stays put once allowed to cool. It is slightly thinner in the middle than it is at the ends rather like a radio rod. It is best to fix rods like this to the model with 'superglue' as opposed to liquid cement which takes some time to dry out.

The only really poor point on the model is the exhaust box guard. It is moulded on the track sprue and is far too thick and 'close'; it looks totally wrong. There are two ways of making a better piece. The first way is to mark out a

Stretching sprue. Hold sprue over a candle and rotate it. When it softens, turns black and begins to smoke, remove it from the flame.

Finally the tracks must be approached. The tracks as supplied with this model are the ultimate development of the crude bands issued with the first generation of model tanks which were, I am sure, a 'play' feature that has unfortunately, become established. Model tracks really needed rethinking some time ago. Realistic hard plastic ones are now becoming available but with most current models we are stuck with the flexible type. Fortunately, Italeri developed flexible tracks to their limits and they are more than acceptable. Indeed they are like most of the kit, of excellent quality. The main snag with these tracks, and

Gently draw it apart.

piece of 10 one-thousandths of an inch (10 thou.) sheet and drill in the holes. The sheet is then cut to size, glued in position at the top and, when dry, bent round the exhaust and fixed to the bottom. This is quite effective but not perhaps the best way as it is very difficult to get the holes even and, besides, the thin sheet distorts. The second method is very much better. A piece of lead foil from a wine bottle is flattened and the kit piece taped over it. The kit item acts as a template, the holes being pushed in the foil with a thick sewing needle. The task can be made even easier if the needle is bound to a handle such as an old, thick paintbrush shaft. This 'tool' is a very useful one indeed, with a multitude of uses for scribing and drilling. An etched brass exhaust cover is available but it is quite expensive and really offers no advantages over the lead foil idea.

indeed with all tracks of this sort, is that they do not 'lie' properly and they never sag along the top run like the real thing. This is doubtless due to the inherent qualities of the material used to make tracks which is strong, flexible, and resilient. Fortunately this sagging may be induced quite easily and, more importantly, rather realistically.

Should the top run be near to the trackguard then pieces of sprue, painted matt black, may be pushed in between the two, forcing the track down and giving a very acceptable impression of 'track sag'. This method will not work if the top run and guard are some way apart. In instances such as these, as for example on this model, the tracks must be held down with a piece of strong rod where each 'sag' is found. This sounds quite complex but in reality it is a simple process using headless pins and some

Induce track sag by drilling and supergluing pins ...

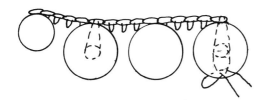

... or by sewing down the tracks over large road wheels.

commonsense. The tracks are trial fitted and then pushed down to see where the 'sag' will occur. The positions of the pins are then marked in and the tracks removed. The pins then have their heads cut off and are held in pliers, heated until they are glowing red and driven into the relevant positions.

A rather more precise method of achieving the same end result would be to drill the holes with a fine modelling drill then epoxy the pins in place. When the model is painted and the track fitted these pins do not show up at all. Finally, if the top run of the track rests directly upon the top of large road wheels, such as on the Russian T34 or the German Panther where there are no return rollers, the track can usually be 'sewn' directly to the road wheels. A loop of thread is put through to top of the track and secured round the central axle of each relevant road wheel, thus holding the track down in position. The figures above show these methods. All these methods work, are relevant to the configuration of the models and, best of

all, they improve the finished appearance of the model no end. It is also possible to 'superglue' down the tracks but this is not quite as permanent as sewing.

OPTIONAL FITTINGS

The model has now been built. However, models built 'from the box' usually lack any real personality. This can be given by adding optional fittings, the stowage *usually* carried and a crew. As always this is largely a matter of personal choice. Some modellers prefer a clean, standard, uncluttered model 'battened down' but in our opinion the models look rather bland uninteresting. A standard fitting on most German tanks of the early war period was a box/cover for the smoke candles mounted on the vehicle's rear plate. On this vehicle it was mounted behind the exhaust. Five tubes containing the smoke candles were mounted on a plate and enclosed at the sides and from above. This fitting was attached to the vehicle by two brackets one positioned over the centre of the exhaust cover and the other, more simple one, to the left of the exhaust assembly. Fittings such as these are relatively simple to fabricate and they improve one's modelling

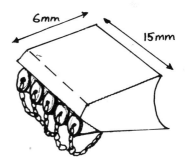

Make up the smoke-candle fitting from 10 thou. plastic card and brass or plastic tubing.

skills immeasurably as well as the finished appearance of the model. Begin by studying the drawings and, if you have any photographs of the vehicle which show the cover study them also. Mark out, using a ruler and set-square, the rear plate on 20 thou. sheet. Cut it out, then mark and cut out the sides from the same material. Fit them together using liquid cement, check for squareness and allow this assembly to dry out.

Cut the top cover from 10 thou. sheet and note that it is necessary to curve the front edge. This is quite easily achieved. Tape the front portion of the piece firmly over a piece of sprue of the relevant diameter. Run this piece under very hot water for about twenty seconds or so and then under cold water for somewhat longer. When removed from the sprue the curve will be permanent and will not spring out. Fit this piece and again, allow to dry out.

The candles can be made from lengths of sprue. Make up the exhaust bracket from 10 thou. as shown and fit it over the exhaust. The other bracket is simply a strip of 10 thou. Fit this bracket to the cover, then fit the whole assembly in position. If necessary, support it with a blob of 'Bluetack' until it has dried out. The covers or caps on the end of the candle tubes were attached to longish chains, presumably to prevent them being lost in action. Even the finest modelling chain looks overscale, so these chains are best depicted by lengths of thread each secured with a dab of contact adhesive. These improvements do show up the model and help lift it out of the ordinary class. Painting and presentation will be tackled in Chapter 2.

THE TAMIYA T34/85

Most modellers in the larger scales 'cut their teeth' on Tamiya models. They generally are of excellent quality, although as a whole they never quite reached the standards of accuracy that Italeri models did at their peak. However, they always look right, are robust, fit together well, and are full of character. The presentation and packaging are always of the highest order and their instruction sheets are the best available, being comprehensive, beautifully illustrated and full of useful hints and tips. Many modellers feel that the T34 series were the finest models this concern ever made and quite comparable to any other model kits. They are notable for accuracy, excellent detail and texture and for exactly capturing the rather brutal appearance of the real thing. The latest model from Tamiya is, oddly enough, of the final version of the tank which was equipped with a larger, more powerful, gun carried in a bigger turret. The kit is well up to standard.

Working method

The T34/85 does, however, require a little more effort than the Panzer I. The prominent joins on the turret, fuel tanks and gun tube need to be concealed, some fittings are missing and there are some features which need to be removed.

CONCEALING JOINS

The turret, fuel tanks and gun tube come moulded in halves and when glued together prominent joins are quite visible. These can be sanded smooth but frequently a 'flat' occurs where the join line once was, usually as a result of too vigorous an action involved in banishing it. The best way to make sure that the joins will not show and that no such unsightly 'flats' result is to join the parts together with liquid plastic. If this is applied generously and the parts squeezed together so that some of the thick solution oozes out from the join it can, when dry, be smoothed down, thus preserving the circular cross section and making the join line vanish. Liquid plastic is

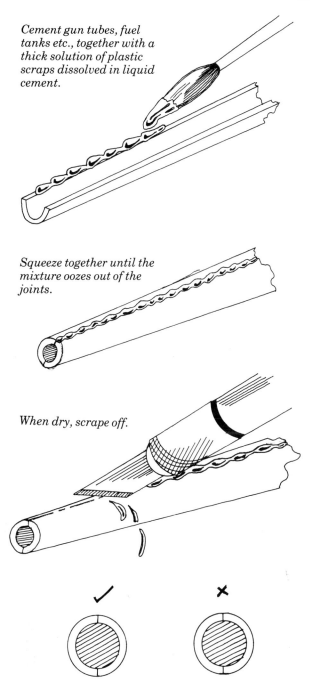

Cement gun tubes, fuel tanks etc., together with a thick solution of plastic scraps dissolved in liquid cement.

Squeeze together until the mixture oozes out of the joints.

When dry, scrape off.

Make sure you end up with a perfectly round section.

easily made by adding small pieces of sprue to liquid cement, shaking vigorously and allowing it to dissolve fully overnight. The thickness of the solution depends entirely on the proportion of sprue added to the cement. This mixture can be used as an adhesive and as a filler. When dry it may be filed, sanded or cut as kit plastic which is a very handy trait. It is best to scrape it off the join areas, when dry, with the edge of a blade then finish off with gentle sanding with a very fine grade of abrasive paper. Where it is needed to take the smoothing operations to a raised edge, such as the strapping on the fuel tanks, a few light strokes with a Swiss file removes the excess filler and preserves the square edge.

The armour-cast texture needs restoring where the joins have been disguised. The texture moulded on the turret is exceptionally effective and it would be a shame to lose it. Before beginning this operation the raised 'blister' on the near side of the turret should be carved off if a wartime vehicle is to be depicted; this bulge seems to have only been found on post-war vehicles of Czech origin. It is a simple matter to carve and file it away without going through the main thickness of plastic. The currently popular method of adding or restoring texture is to 'bounce' a modelling electric drill on its slow setting over the area to be treated. This is quite effective but there are other equally good ways of achieving the same result. One of the best is to moisten the area with strong liquid cement and press a piece of coarse sandpaper against it, firmly, until it dries. When the sandpaper is peeled away its texture is left behind imprinted into the plastic. Another method is again to moisten the area with strong cement then dab away at the area with a stiff bristled brush until the area begins to 'set off'. All these methods are a little messy and practice on an old (and unloved) model is strongly recommended before the latest acquisition is attacked.

Modifications made to the Tamiya T34/85, showing the turret weld seams (overemphasized) and texture as well as the battered trackguards.

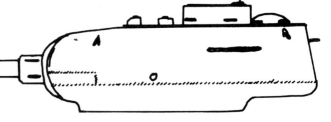

Make up the new weld seams from thin strips of 10 thou. Add 'welded' texture with a hot knife blade.

ADDING DETAIL

The T34/85 turrets were cast in two separate halves which were then welded together, the welded joint being very prominent and, contrariwise as usual, much more prominent than that in the kit. The best way of depicting these weld lines is to cement *very* thin and long strips of 10 thou. sheet in their positions. The welded texture may be added by gently dabbing the strip with a heated craft-knife blade. Use an old blade, heat it to dull red and very gently dab the strip along its length until the blade is too cool to mark the plastic; reheat it and continue. Again practice is highly recommended. The trackguard ends on the real vehicles inevitably soon became battered, and this feature can be reproduced upon the model. Gently heat the guards over a small candle flame, keeping them moving so that the flame does not dwell upon one area too long; when the plastic becomes malleable, use the end of a paintbrush handle to make the dents which indicate damage.

Hinge detail can be added to the inside of the hatches from slivers of thin sheet and the racking and 'plumbing' for the rear plate/hull fuel tanks made up, as shown, from strips of 10 thou. sheet and plastic rod.

Another nice touch is to add a rough texture

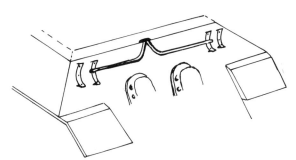

Make these fuel pipes from thin plastic or brass rod. Make the tank mounting brackets from 10 thou. strip.

The finished model. The markings are hand-painted. Note how the weathering helps to 'define' the model and how the crew figures bring it to life.

to the running surfaces of the road wheel tyres. The mould marks on them are quite noticeable and should be removed, preferably with a piece of rough sandpaper. The resultant rough texture depicts wear and tear on the (supposedly) rubber surface very well indeed.

If the model is to be shown opened up it is essential to paint and fit the driver figure before the hull top is fitted to the chassis pan. The question of AFV crews will be discussed at the end of the section.

The net result should be a model of the very highest quality. It does involve a little effort if the best is to be had from this model, but the end product is well worth it.

THE TAMIYA M3 GRANT

Everyone has an off day and this model proves that the designers who were responsible were no exception. The complex shape of the turret is captured to perfection, as is the overall appearance of the vehicle. However, the sandguards are far too thick and clumsy. Worst of all, however, are the tracks. They appear to have been copied directly from those of the Monogram Grant/Lee models which were completely wrong. On the real vehicles the individual track links were joined to each other with standard end connectors which also combined the guide horns. Thus each connector

joined up two links; on the Monogram model they were depicted as being attached to the individual links. This mistake should never have happened but what was quite unforgivable on Tamiya's model was that this very obvious mistake was copied. The tracks simply looked nonsensical – there was no way in which they could have worked and/or stayed together on the real vehicle. What made matters even worse was that one hobby magazine tried to excuse this error by stating

An elderly Grant kit from Tamiya having been rescued. Note the new tracks, sandshields and added texture to the turret.

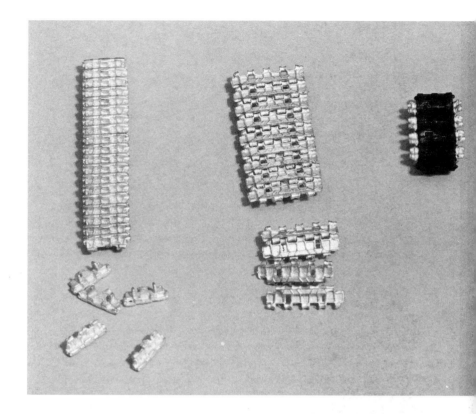

Many manufacturers are making strenuous efforts to provide modellers with more realistic tracks, since the soft plastic types have never been regarded as ideal. From left to right they are: the 'link and length' type, available in resin, plastic and, as here, metal (Accurate Armour); individual links in metal, as here, or plastic (Peddinghaus); and three-piece links in plastic and metal – an excellent solution, though tedious to assemble (Top Brass).

that it might be impossible to mould the tracks in their correct configuration. This statement was just as daft as the original mistake. The final reason for most modellers' unhappiness with this model was the complete lack of texture on the turret's surface; in real life the turret has a texture akin to rough sponge – neat it most certainly was not!

I might have taken a milder view of the faults inherent in the kit had the model in question been an early effort. Sadly this was not the case; this is a third generation model released about the same time as some really outstanding items. Fortunately there is a brighter side to all this, especially as a supporting 'cottage industry' now exists. It is, in fact, a fairly simple task to turn the model into a first-class miniature.

Working method
Assemble basic model as per the kit instructions, disregarding the sandshields. Texture can be added to the turret in any number of ways as discussed in the previous project; I used the rough side of a pedicure hard-skin remover. This tool is, in effect, a miniature cheese-vegetable grater and several strokes with it transform the most unblemished surface into a heavily textured one.

FITTING NEW TRACKS AND SANDSHIELDS
Next the chassis and running gear are painted prior to fitting the new tracks. It seems that if some items are substandard in the model world then some enterprising concern will provide replacement parts. It is now possible to buy

Rear inner side.

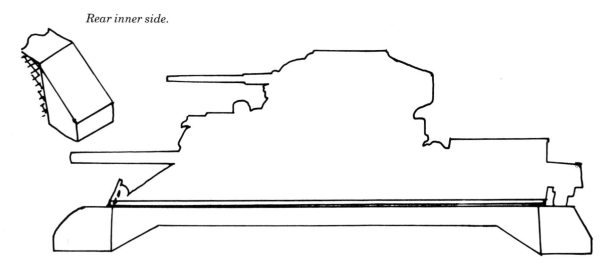

New trackguards for the Grant.

replacement tracks for most popular, early models. One company, Top Brass, make three types of M3/M4 'medium' pattern tracks including an early, three-bar, type. Individual links and metal guide horn/connectors are provided and the tracks made up from these individual units. It is a fairly long process but the results are quite good, and comprehensive instructions are provided with the tracks. There is another rather cheaper, much easier and equally good solution to the problem, which is to use the tracks from the Italeri M4. The kit itself is cheaper than the track kit and is far easier to obtain. The tracks are of the early pattern ideal for the Grant/Lee and they are very well reproduced. Although this means scrapping a kit once all the useful parts have been put in the spares box it is a cheap and logical way to replace the Tamiya horrors! As a point of interest, when I first purchased the kit several years ago I scratch built new tracks: they were quite an easy pattern to make up.

The tracks should now be painted and fitted, and attention may be turned to the sand-shields. These are best made from 10 thou. sheet and the kit items may be used as a template. There were several patterns of trackguard, and I used a less usual type. Note that the front ends are squared off and that the rear ends are also of a different type. 10 thou. is the best material for this sort of task and it is quite sturdy whilst giving an excellent impression of 'scale thinness'. It is easy to cut and work and its very lack of thickness virtually guarantees a sharp edge. The only real snag with this material is that it distorts fairly easily if cut with too much gusto or if large areas are left unsupported.

As the kit upper trackguard/forward upper portion of the trackguard is to be used, it is necessary to square off the front end. Mark off, in pencil, the portions to be removed from the parts. Cutting through the thick kit plastic is not nearly such a difficult task as might be thought but it does need some care. It is practically mandatory to use the steel rule as a cutting guide and holding it up against this curved (and suddenly slippery) surface seems to become a difficult task! In instances like this I usually tape the rule firmly in position. Never try to get through the plastic all in one cut.

Instead, make the first cut a gentle one, apply slightly more pressure to the second cut and only very little more to the third. The parts may simply snap off at the scored lines; a few strokes with a file or emery board will soon clean up any unevenness. When making the side pieces it is best to cut out rectangles of sheet to the overall size. In this instance they are 14 by 165 mm (½ in. by 6½ in.) When cutting through any sheet, even of this limited thickness, always use several gentle cuts as opposed to one brutal one; not only will the parts come out undistorted but the blade points will last that much longer. Once these parts are cut and checked against each other to make sure that they are *exactly* the same, the bottom edge 'cut outs' should be marked in and removed. The new rear parts can be made up from 20 thou., as the greater thickness of this stronger material will not be apparent on the finished model. The side pieces can now be fitted, using a minimum of cement, and when the whole assembly has dried out they may be trimmed to shape.

The Grant finished in plain sand as delivered to the troops. It is correct in configuration, unlike the basic kit.

FITTINGS AND ACCESSORIES

The M3/M4 'mediums' have spawned a host of accessories and fittings kits/sets. These fitting sets are sheets of etched brass containing 'scale thickness' items such as headlamp and periscope guards, tools, straps, brackets, etc. If properly fitted they do enhance the finished appearance on any model but they seem a rather complex, over the top and expensive way of solving a minor modelmaking dilemma. The headlamp guards in the kit are far too thick but are very easily replaced with ones fabricated from 10 thou. strip. The moulded-on strapping can be trimmed from the tools and replaced with paper straps, and with buckles from Historex (the French miniature-figure manufacturer) if one feels that small squares of sheet are not really up to depicting these items (I think that they are). The sun shield rails can be cut from pre-sliced strip sheet polystyrene (microstrip) and fitted.

Next all the rivets have to be fitted to the new parts. Making model rivets is not one of the better aspects of the hobby. The task is repetitive, boring and nearly always frustrating. More than one model has nearly come to grief when a previously unsuspected area is found to be devoid of vital rivets. The simple fact is that it *is* essential to depict riveted detail. It is very visible and most conspicuous by its absence. It is possible to carve rivets off an old kit but the usual method is to cut thin slices of plastic rod, put a dab of liquid cement in each position then pick up a slice/rivet on the tip of the craft knife and put it in place.

Some join lines need depicting on the sandshield sides. This is best done by scoring them in, very gently, with a needle. It is far better to carry out this operation at this stage even though it might appear simpler to do it before the parts are fitted. The advantage of doing it when the sandshields are fitted is that they are much less likely to distort.

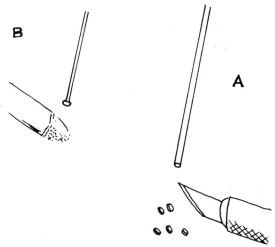

Cut rivets from rod, as in A, or hold rod near a heat source, such as a lighted cigar or soldering iron head, until it 'mushrooms' (B). Cut off behind the head and drill a hole to take the rivet. Secure in both instances with a wash of cement.

Fill in the locating holes for the tools and sand them smooth; then remove the loop ends of the tow cable before throwing it away with the kit tracks. These ends are fitted to a length of thick carpet thread using contact adhesive. The thread can be given a more acceptable finish by painting with liquid plastic made by dissolving scrap plastic in liquid cement. An alternative material would be brass picture wire which is a miniature of the real thing. In effect, it is however, a little more difficult to form.

Facing page top: *The high standard of current kits is well illustrated by this Italeri Chaffee in 1/35th scale with a mix of commercial figures. Model by Erik Johansen.*

Bottom: *The same model fitted with Top Brass detailing kit and white metal tracks. Note the extensive animation allowed for by these tracks and the heavy weathering. Model by Paul Williams.*

The main gun mantlet dust cover can then be fitted. The best thing to use for this sort of piece is good-quality facial tissue. Using *sharp* household scissors, cut a long strip of tissue to width, then into sections as shown below. Using contact adhesive, glue it, one side at a time, about the hull barbette. Prod and push it into position using a pencil or similar. Once it is fitted to the hull end and trimmed, soak it in a thin solution of white PVA glue and water, then 'gather' it about the gun tube. If necessary, secure the end with a dab of full strength PVA. When dry, the tissue will be found to be remarkably tough and have an excellent surface for painting.

Both upper hatches can be replaced with ones cut from 20 thou. which look very much more 'scalish'. Hinge detail and a periscope

Canvas dust cover. Cut pieces from tissue as shown in A. Fit as described and wash with water/white glue solution to give the effect in B.

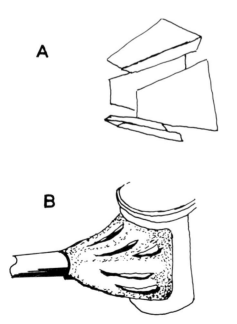

bottom are added from scraps of strip and kit plastic.

Finally, the very conspicuous stowage is added. The main bundle is made from a few wads of tissue well wrapped up inside several layers of the same material. It is tied to the sunshield rail with thread, then the thread is covered, where relevant, with paper 'strapping'. The bundle is then soaked in the PVA solution and prodded into shape. It should look decidedly casual. Stowage for the other side consists of a smaller bundle, several Italeri accessory small packs, and helmets. Whilst these can be glued directly onto the rail, care has to be taken to ensure that they do not look like anti-gravity packs by fitting paper straps and making sure that they show.

Plenty of other stowage, fitted anywhere that there was room, seems to have been a feature of these vehicles in the desert. Fortunately the Grant was an extremely well photographed vehicle, so many ideas for individualizing one's own model are readily available.

A lovely final touch to the model is one of those exquisite Verlindin 30 cal. machine guns. It really sets off the model, even if a great deal of patience is needed to make it up. This is one type of accessory of which I do approve.

This all sounds like a great deal of effort expended upon a kit which is not as good as it might have been to begin with. However, all the faults in the kit are easily corrected and the end result is a model that will stand comparison with any. It is also a subject with real, if rugged, character. Never be put off by a model which looks dated or heavy in comparison with the latest releases. Providing that the model is basically right it can be worked up to a high standard and will ensure, when finished, a great deal more satisfaction than building something 'straight from the box'.

FURTHER THOUGHTS ON KITS

I hope I have made the point that no kits are beyond improvement. Successful and advanced modellers always treat a model kit as only the minimal basis of a miniature of the real thing. Never believe that the manufacturers have 'done it all', equally, it should never be beyond one's ability to correct the mistakes that the manufacturers have made, and they should never be ignored if they are known.

Limitations in the plastic moulding process, however, cannot be blamed upon the poor manufacturers. Many parts cannot be moulded to scale thickness even though the quality of moulding has improved greatly of late. An example is the skirting armour fitted to many German AFVs during the later period of the Second World War. The purpose of this armour was to detonate hollow-charge ammunition a safe distance away from the thin hull sides. Late Panzer IVs were also fitted with an apron of this armour around the turret (as were, in fact, the final versions of the Panzer III). This gave the vehicles a very distinctive appearance. The kit versions are far too thick and rigid; in real life the skirts were about as flimsy as trackguards and were easily damaged, especially the front ones. The best thing to do is to use the kit items as a pattern and cut fresh ones from 10 thou. sheet. They can easily be twisted, distorted or battered with the application of a little heat as described previously. The turret aprons may be fabricated in similar fashion and the relevant curve can be put in the sheet simply by pulling it under a ruler pressed firmly down upon it. Do this a couple of times and the sheet will have assumed the required curvature. An even better effect can be had if one is prepared to fabricate the stays and arms upon which this stand-off armour was hung. It is a task requiring some patience but it gives a very realistic appearance.

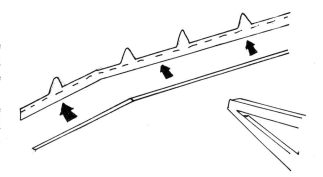

Make up Schurtzen armour brackets from 10 thou., as shown, using kit parts as pattern to give scale-thickness effect.

Another unusual finish sported by German tanks of this vintage was the Zimmerit anti-magnetic paste which was applied in an attempt to stop infantry attaching magnetic mines to them during close combat. There are several variants of finish of this paste due to the various methods of application but the most familiar one is a series of regularly spaced small ridges. This effect may be engraved into the surface of the model using a soldering iron fitted with a fine point but this is quite a 'final' method — if a mistake is made you are stuck with it! Far and away the best idea is to cover the surface, a small area at a time, with a thin layer of filler. Fit an old blade to the craft knife (a curved one is best), and spread a fresh blob of filler, about the size of a small pea, in a thin layer as far as it will go. It is best to try to apply it to a distinct area such as the driver's plate or a turret side, removing any surplus. It is nearly impossible to spread this material in an even layer but once it is roughly applied the blade may be wiped clean, dipped in soapy water then used to pat the layer smooth.

Two tools are very useful for embossing the pattern into the filler. The main one is a fine comb, or, best of all, a toothcomb. The other tool is a small screwdriver. Again, dip the tools into water to prevent the filler sticking and, if necessary, break the comb into smaller pieces so that it can be fitted into tight spots and pressed right to the edge of the turret etc. The screwdriver can produce the embossing about the machine-gun blisters, edges of the mantlet and so on. If demarcation lines are required as was sometimes the case on the real thing, then they may simply be pressed in with the back edge of the blade. Zimmerit seems to have chipped very easily and photographs show a decidedly less than fully covered vehicle with large patches missing. These patches are best cut out before the filler has fully cured; carefully cut out the shape, scrape away the filler, then attend to the edges. Do not worry about leaving a slight residue on the missing area, as this was what happened with real Zimmerit.

An embossed plastic sheet depicting this type of surface is currently available. Although it at first appears to be a rather complex solution to a simple modelling matter it is quite a good product well worth investigating. It gives a fairly good overall effect but it is a little too smooth looking. Representing chipping, however, would simply be a matter of cutting out the relevant areas and the material has the great advantage that it can be applied during construction when the model is in component form.

Specialist kits

Specialist kits are, by and large, made for enthusiasts by enthusiasts. As such they are usually of the less commercial subjects, are accurate and more expensive than plastic kits. It is only fair to point out that the quality varies; whilst some of the models are poor, the best are at least as good as their injection-moulded relations.

The reason for the high cost of these models is the considerable expense of the moulding materials plus the fact that they are not manufactured in large quantities. The moulds themselves also need replacing at regular intervals.

As noted before, the kits are usually very accurate as they are well researched and the patterns made by keen modelmakers. Indeed sometimes it seems that the kit makers are trying to cram in an excessive number of features.

There are four approaches to the provision of specialist, or rather enthusiasts', kits. These are 'hi-tech' kits, resin kits (now with a frequent and increasing metal content), metal kits, and vacuum-moulded kits.

HI-TECH KITS

The Gunze Sangyo PZ III J

These should be the Rolls-Royce of kits – they certainly cost an equivalent price. The one discussed here cost about six times that of its Tamiya equivalent and, at first, seems comparatively poor value. Upon opening the box, however, one's first impression is of sheer quality of the parts, the excellent packing and the very comprehensive instructions. Whilst the basic kit is in white plastic many parts are cast in very high-quality white metal, others are etched brass, and the gun tubes are in turned brass. The track links are individual 'snap together' mouldings, a near perfect solution. The fit of parts is very good, the quality of the parts outstanding and there seems to be virtually no way that one can improve upon the model. In point of fact the sheer quality of the kit is nearly hypnotic – one begins to believe that nothing can be wrong with a kit like this. 'Sez who?' There is something wrong with it, quite a big something, which points at simple carelessness by the manufacturer.

This kit is supposed to depict an Ausf J. model vehicle. This was the last basic version of the vehicle produced. Whilst there were later models, the tank was really past its best. These later models were really modifications of the 'J' simplified, given some extra protection or fitted with a close-support gun. Whilst the kit is accurate as a 'J' in most respects, the rear engine decking is the simplified pattern of an 'L' model or later. From the amount of detail packed into the kit it is obvious that it was based upon the very close study of a preserved vehicle. My opinion is that the vehicle in question was the one preserved in the Royal Armoured Corps museum at Bovington. This is an early 'L' version without the spaced armour but with some of the supporting frames fitted,

The hi-tech Pz III, showing the corrections needed to the rear decking.

so it might have been mistaken for an earlier variant. (In fact it now seems that the model might have been based on a vehicle preserved in Norway, which was subsequently fitted with a new engine-deck from a later pattern.)

Understanding how the mistake was made does not mean that it is acceptable or forgivable, however. All that was needed was for the basic information to be cross-referenced with any of the large number of published drawings or the masses of photographic evidence available. Measuring up the real thing always seems to be the one and only foolproof method of getting exact, first-hand information. In fact it is a method fraught with difficulties. Most people have seen items in museums wrongly labelled. Curators are frequently well qualified in one particular field but have limited knowledge of other aspects and they may not know if a vehicle is wrong. Museum exhibits were often captured during hostilities and may well have been captured in a damaged state and repaired with parts of an even more damaged vehicle. Sometimes two vehicles are even combined to make one whole one. Simple cross-referencing would have given the relevant information.

WORKING METHOD

Correcting the mistake is not too difficult an exercise. The raised locating walls on the engine access panels can be smoothed down, then the apertures blocked from underneath with 40 thou. plastic sheet. The gaps are filled with the same material as snugly as possible, then finished off with filler. Once the gap has been smoothed the 'split' in the main hatches is scribed in.

As the air intake covers are too big, new ones can be made from rectangles of 40 thou. sheet carefully rubbed to shape. They are mounted on smaller rectangles of 20 thou. then fitted in place (see page 41, top). Four new hinges must be made, two per hatch. It is quite possible to make them up from scratch but it is equally easy to mould your own. Simple Plasticine is the basic mouldmaking material for a not too demanding mould of this nature. Make up a smooth, flat piece of Plasticine at least 50 mm (2 in.) square. Spray the surface with powdered graphite (obtainable from hardware stores as a lock lubricant), then press the kit hinges into the surface. Carefully pick them out using the point of a blade, and make four more moulds as some of the first four may not work. The moulding compound used in this case is fast-setting epoxy resin, a batch being made up

and dripped into each mould from a pointed matchstick. When dry they are removed, the backs sanded flat and then the best ones fitted.

New rear intake covers can be made up from 40 thou. sheet and fitted, as those supplied are far too large. The long gun tube supplied is also far too long, although the short one is accurate. If you intend to fit the long gun, then the end 10 mm (2/5 in.) must be sawn off, the new end smoothed and redrilled. This is quite a task, especially for those used to working in plastic, but it can be done.

Finally, do beware of the instructions. At first they seem to be most comprehensive but, at times, they are rather vague as regards locations. There are few location holes, marks, etc., on the kit so the instructions should be more exact. Fortunately, many references exist on the Pz III and as the model is likely to appeal only to the committed or advanced modelmaker, this is not such a problem as it might have been. I found the Squadron/Signal *PxKpfw III in Action* an invaluable reference.

RESIN KITS

Kits made from this material have been with us for several years and are currently enjoying a very high profile.

The first kits of this type that I recall were the splendid range (in 1/76th scale) introduced by Eric Clark and available exclusively to the

Facing page top: *The finished model is impressive if corrected, but better might be expected from such an expensive kit.*

Bottom: *A selection of good-quality resin cast conversion kits. Top: the Cromwell 1/35-scale PzIV L70 Zwischen Lözung tank destroyer and Verlinden Crusader conversion; bottom left: the Al-By Churchill mk IV tank/engineer vehicle conversion; bottom right: a selection of Cromwell alternative turrets for various 1/76th-scale kits, including three for the T34.*

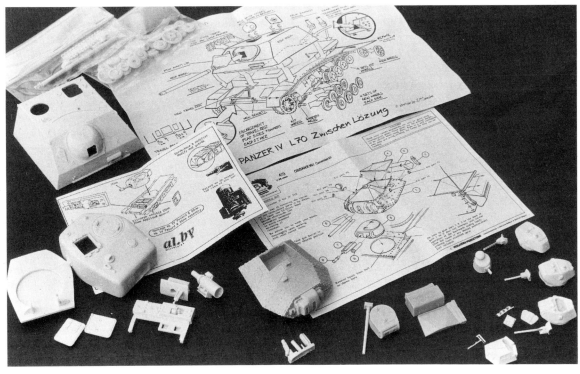

members of the Miniature Armoured Fighting Vehicles Association (MAFVA). The idea of these was that they should supplement the existing models, which were then a little thin on the ground, by making available the less commercial types. Manufactured by smaller concerns at the cottage-industry end of the scale, these models represent two extremes of the craft: at their very best they are simply unbeatable; at their worst, quite dreadful!

The models begin life as a highly detailed master built using the methods detailed in the scratch building section. Obviously, nearly everything depends upon the skill of the master maker, but as these models are, by and large, made by enthusiasts for enthusiasts, the standards are very high indeed. Moulds, in silicon rubber, are taken from the masters and the models are cast off in high-definition resin. This method of manufacture allows a very high degree of detail to be incorporated – a level which no other process can match. An advantageous by-product of the process is that fewer parts are required for the complete model and this simplifies construction.

Although the tooling costs involved in setting up such a model for manufacture are tiny in comparison with those of a plastic injection-moulded kit, the resin itself is very expensive; moreover, the moulds do not last for long and therefore need replacing frequently, and there is a high percentage of mismoulded parts which must be discarded. Manufacture is a slow and labour-intensive business and the models will never sell in really large numbers. All of these factors account for the high price of the products.

British and European models currently enjoy the highest reputation. This is mainly due to the fact that they are moulded in materials which are unavailable to North American manufacturers; but the quality of products from the States is steadily improving.

From the above remarks it will be obvious that a poor model will cost just as much as an excellent one. Before buying a kit, try and find out as much about it as possible. Magazine reviews are a good starting-point, but the best source of all is the opinion of experienced modellers – another good reason for joining your local modelling society. If a chance to examine a kit is possible the things to look for are as follows. Good packaging protects the model and is an important, if frequently overlooked, factor. Good instructions are equally important, since there is no point buying a model then having to spend a couple of months finding out how it fits together! The most important factor of all is the obvious one. Examine the quality of the moulding as regards its crispness, texture, standard of detail and freedom from moulding flaws.

The reputation of some model-making houses is perhaps the safest guarantee of quality: the best ones simply don't make a sub-standard model. David and I have had the opportunity of examining models from nearly all the manufacturers and in our carefully considered opinion can recommend the following models without hesitation.

In 1/76th scale, Cromwell models are in a class of their own.

In 1/35th scale, models by Accurate Armour, Al-by, NKC Products, Dartmoor Models and Verlinden are of the highest standards. Slightly behind these are items from MB Models, Des Models and ADV Models – the latter concern's products originating from the United States. They are slightly 'woolly' as compared with the best but all are full of character – at least as good as plastic kits – and will not disappoint.

The efforts of a few makers left both of us feeling dazed: some offered rubbish; some turned out excellent models alongside very indifferent pieces; whilst one British firm infuriated us by offering beautifully made models which were weak in terms of accuracy.

One of the most famous of all the British post-war armoured vehicles is the Ferret armoured car. They have served almost everywhere with all branches of the service, and are instantly familiar to European modellers. It seems, however, that major manufacturers have shied away from producing kits of Ferrets. As a less 'glamorous' vehicle type, it is unlikely they would sell in sufficient quantities to be a viable economic proposition. This is just the sort of situation that the smaller manufacturers are able to exploit, and have moved in to provide such models at a price which the keen modeller or collector is willing to pay.

As there are, at the time of writing, three manufacturers offering this model, it seems like a good idea to see how each have tackled the subject.

The better resin-cast models are made by enthusiasts for enthusiasts, and tend to be very accurate and finely detailed. Larger-scale models, such as Accurate Armour's Scimitar, feature parts in metal and etched brass. These small-scale models from Cromwell feature an incredible amount of detail.

Cromwell Models: Ferret Armoured Car Mk 1/2 (1/76th scale)

By way of a change I broke away from my usual 1/35th scale and made up the two variants of the vehicle offered by Cromwell models in 1/76th scale. This firm produces rather more than 150 models and has the reputation of being one of the very best manufacturers of small-scale models, and I would completely agree with this assessment. The kits involved are the Ferrets Mks 1 and 2. The basic difference between the two is that the Mk 1 is an open-topped vehicle principally used for liaison duties whilst the Mk 2 sports a small machine-gun-armed turret and is used in the light-reconnaissance role.

The kits themselves are simple to assemble as they consist of very few parts, the quality of which is impressive. The basic hull consists of two parts, the main hull/chassis and the fighting-compartment roof. As both parts are hollow this enables the model to be depicted 'opened up' as is usual with the real vehicle.

A pair of ferrets in 1/76th scale from Cromwell. These tiny models carry the same amount of detail as a decent 1/35th-scale kit and, being very simple to assemble, are ideal if you want to try out resin kits.

Vision flaps are moulded separately with detail upon both sides. (Other kit-makers take note!) The suspension units are moulded onto the wheels and are beautifully detailed. The other few parts are equally impressive. The fact which immediately strikes one is the amount of detail incorporated into the model, bearing in mind its tiny size. This amount of detail would not disgrace a good large-scale kit as I hope the photograph reveals.

Mould marks and their associated 'flash' (this is where the moulding material has 'crept' between the mould halves, producing a very fine membrane) are easily sanded or cut off. The resin is very malleable and does not shatter, unlike the first types of resin. Any small air bubbles which may appear on the outer surfaces of the model are easily filled –

this I did by forcing a little Greenstuff filler into them with a pointed matchstick. When the filler dried, I sanded it smooth with a fine grade of abrasive paper. All told, preparation of each kit took about an hour and assembly perhaps a fifth as long. The results of that brief modelling session were two small-scale models of the highest quality. Despite their tiny size, they are so beautifully made that they seem to possess what I can only describe as a jewel-like quality. They cost about two to three times the price of an equivalent plastic kit, but represent very good value for money if quality is your main consideration. I have to admit that since making up these two items I have bought more Cromwell Models and am working my way through them.

Military Miniature Models: Ferret Mk 1/2 (1/35th scale)

When we first had the idea for this book this was one of the first models I sought out. In fact I was going to built a Ferret from scratch, and the kit promised to save me the bother! Unfortunately the kit is no longer with us, having recently been withdrawn, but as it represented for me, a first-generation effort it is worth looking at briefly.

Theoretically, the model could be made up either as a Mk 1 or 2. In fact, this was a piece of fiction, no matter how charitable a view one was prepared to take, as the two parts of the hull could only be constructed into a solid unit. Only a comprehensive engineering exercise could have made an opening. And as the Mk 1 is an open-topped vehicle … some modellers might have been prepared to accept this and depict the open hull top by painting it matt black; but, given the model's cost (about three times that of the equivalent plastic kit), I did not really think this course was acceptable. An unfortunate by-product of the Ferret's 'identity crisis' was that the combings on the hull top

needed to be removed before the turreted version could be tackled – with the resulting danger that some damage could occur.

The quality of the model was quite good but very basic for a kit in this scale. The suspension arms were crude and some of the accessory parts, notably the sand channel, ammunition box and cable reel, were so badly moulded that they were unusable. The kit was a mixture of resin and white metal parts, and though most of the mouldings were quite crisp, some of the metal parts showed signs of damage where they had been removed from the sprues. The worst feature of the model was its lack of definition. Some parts were very well detailed but others lacked any. Some tools and fittings were missing and there were no lashing eyes on the turret, which are features immediately apparent on the real vehicle. I made up these parts from fine fuse wire and other fittings from paper or thin plastic card. As the *basis* for a model it was fine, but fell disappointingly short of my high expectations.

The annoying thing about the kit is that the master was made by John Bottomley, who is an extremely talented modeller. I have had the chance to examine some of his masters that are now being produced by another concern, and they are really first-rate. Possibly the lack of quality is explained by inexperience on the manufacturer's part, and as an early effort it is, perhaps, forgivable.

Dartmoor Models: Ferret Mk 2 (1/35th scale)

In contrast with my views about the previous offering, two friends of mine both enthused over the Dartmoor product. As they are model manufacturers themselves, and as I consider the range of kits they make to be the very best in their respective scales, I tend to take good notice of their opinions. I obtained a model and my first impressions were most favourable.

The model is well packaged and comes complete with very comprehensive instructions, a nice touch being a couple of three-quarter-view drawings showing the usual stowage arrangements for the vehicle. The bulk of the model is beautifully cast in resin and the wheels and fittings in white metal. These parts are cast to quite the highest standard that I have ever handled. A sign of the thought which has gone into this model was the inclusion of the vehicle-lifting brackets, which are pre-formed from fine-gauge hard wire. The only negative point which struck me immediately was that the body of the vehicle is a one-piece solid casting. The same thing, therefore, applies to this kit as the last one: it is virtually impossible to 'open up'. (I suspect, however, that this factor is irrelevant to most armoured vehicle modellers, who appear to model their vehicles 'closed down'). Further examination of the parts revealed that the *complete* machine gun provided had been based upon an imaginative as opposed to an accurate source, as regards the breech area. As this part is hidden inside the turret it matters not at all; but it is interesting to note that the vehicle manufaturer's drawings show exactly the same speculative gun breech. They were doubtless prepared by an illustrator rather than a draughtsman!

Anyone who has assembled several plastic models will have no difficulty whatever in putting this item together. Models of wheeled vehicles are generally somewhat simpler to put together than those of tracked vehicles and this factor no doubt helps. No flashing was apparent on the parts and the mould marks were easily sanded off. It is best to take a few precautions when sanding a fairly large resin model such as this as the dust raised is easily breathed in and this might not be too good for your lungs. I always use 'wet and dry' abrasive paper, and before beginning to sand I wet the paper in water containing a few drops of liquid soap. This keeps the dust under control and is a far better idea than wearing a face mask. Also try and make sure that your working area is well ventilated and not being used by anyone else. When sanding operations are finished, the paper can either be thrown out or washed free of dust and reused. The same comments apply to filing and sanding white metal parts.

All told, the kit went together beautifully with no problems encountered. The construction of the model coincided with my discovery of a really first-rate 'super glue', MFA Cyano-glue, available from the better type of model outlet. An equally good one is Zap, which is perhaps more widely available – especially in the United States. Using one of these adhesives makes assembling the model a pleasure rather than a chore. The finished result is very impressive as the photograph of the (unpainted) model should show. Where there is detail on the real vehicle it is faithfully depicted on the model. The scale appears to be fairly accurate, although one or two of the angles are perhaps a little suspect. On balance, this model is in the same class as the products of Accurate Armour, Al-by and Cromwell, and they do not come any better than that.

At the time of writing, the Ferret is the only model available from this firm, the next one due being the British Saracen armoured personnel carrier. Evidently this model is not yet in production because demand for the Ferret has been so great that Dartmoor Models is working at full capacity in order to satisfy it.

Facing page top: *The Military Miniature Models Ferret, shown here with the additions I felt to be essential. It is a pleasant enough model but a little basic.* Bottom: *This Dartmoor Ferret is in a different class from the previous offerings.*

A model of a fairly simple vehicle (like the above) is always a good starting point when your project involves the use of unfamiliar materials, such as resin and metal. Besides being straightforward to build, they tend to be considerably less expensive than their more complex, tracked relatives. The sheer quality of the Cromwell and Dartmoor models means that it is quite probable you will find yourself, as I did, 'hooked' upon this type of kit. The reverse side of the coin is that if your first purchase is a 'dud' then it will probably also be your last, so do read the model reviews and find out what experienced modellers make of your particular choice. The best idea of all, however, is to go along to a large modelling show where trade stands will be present. At such an event, you will almost certainly be able to examine the kit itself, and you might be lucky enough to find that the manufacturers have a stand. As I remarked in the preface to this section, those models are made by *aficionados* of the subject – and they will enjoy showing you the models and discussing them.

Al-by Miniatures Renault Char BI bis

Al-by models have always been regarded as the aristocrats of large-scale resin models. They were the first high-quality items and set the standards that the others have had to follow. Made in France, they can be easily obtained and are competitively priced, costing about four to five times the price of an equivalent-sized model from Japan.

The instructions are a little basic. It is just as well that there are few parts to the kit and that assembly is practically self-explanatory. The parts are crisp and well detailed and the tracks are especially good.

The Al-By Char B1. These models set the standards in their day and are still most impressive.

WORKING METHOD

Oddly enough, this model is built from the top down, so no floor plate is provided. I confess that I was uneasy about this as it is always easier to get a model 'true' if working from the bottom up. In this instance the caution proved well founded as some of the parts were slightly warped. This warping is very easy to cure: simply immerse the parts in very hot water until they become malleable, then gently correct them by applying pressure. Once they are right, plunge them into a bowl of cold water. When the tracks are being fitted they can be made to follow the 'track lines' by being heated with a hair dryer and, when soft, being swiftly fixed in position with superglue. It is best to fit the driving sprocket first and the idler last as there is some scope for adjustment with this part which ensures well-fitting tracks.

The rest of the model virtually snaps together; however, it is always best to check for warpage, as this material does seem to suffer somewhat in this respect. Fortunately, remedial action is easy and effective. A really nice touch is the provision of transfers/decals which are as good as any available.

Other kits of French manufacture that I have seen are of equal quality. The choice of subject is, if a little esoteric, just right for the type of modeller who is advancing beyond what is available in the larger retail outlets.

The Accurate Armour Luchs

This kit is very much a 'modeller's model' and, as such, it represents the top end of the resin-kit market. It is a model of a rather rare, specialized German reconnaissance tank. Only a hundred or so were produced and indeed only fifty saw service, the others being cannibalized for spares. Even though these vehicles were rare they were well known and recorded and

students of German armour find them fascinating. For these reasons the vehicle is the perfect subject for a specialized model of this nature.

The kit may be regarded as 'state of the art' as far as resins are concerned. The packaging is very protective which is just as well as the models are usually bought direct from the makers and must travel therefore through the post.

The resin used in these kits is actually sharper than all but the very best injection-moulded plastic and it does not suffer from 'dimpling' or release marks to the same extent. The moulds used are of a latex material and need renewing at regular intervals if standards are to be kept. This, plus the high price of the resin, helps explain the cost of the kit which is about five or six times as high as its plastic equivalent. Although most of the model is cast in resin the tracks, drive sprocket, rims and 20 mm gun tube are cast in white metal.

The instructions are good and inspire confidence. The quality of parts is outstandingly good and this immediately makes a good impression. Some trimming is required to remove 'flash' and mould marks but no more so than in a normal plastic kit. Air bubbles are a little more of a problem but fortunately, due to the way the parts are moulded, they mostly occur on under surfaces where they will not be noticed. Any which show are best filled and sanded smooth.

The fit of the parts is good and the model has been well planned in order that this should be so. The way the model fits together has also been well thought out. Trial fittings of parts is essential to make sure that everything comes together true and square; on models of this nature it is best to take nothing for granted and check before gluing. Besides ensuring a better model, this helps protect a fairly substantial investment.

*The Accurate Armour Luchs under construction,
with some added stowage and an empty jerry-can
rack on the far side of the turret. Fitting the wheels at
a later stage allows them to be painted properly.*

WORKING METHOD
The kit is very accurate with the exception of
the left-hand (seen from the front) shock
absorbers which are mounted the wrong way.
These items were made to one pattern in real
life and, as such, there were no specific
nearside/offside ones; they were therefore
mounted in opposite ways on the different
sides. The offending parts are easily removed
with a razor saw and file and new ones made
up from rod and sheet; as they are partially
covered by the suspension only the top halves
need be made to exact standards.

Assembly is quite straightforward, helped no
end by clear instructions and scrap drawings.

To anyone familiar with plastic kit assembly
there are no real problems over the main
construction. Some difficulty may be experienced with the tracks. You may need to use a
file to make them fit together easily and
square. When making up the front portion it is
best to fit the inner toothed drive rim to the
resin inner, fit the individual links, then add
the outer rim.

Plenty of fittings are provided but as the
vehicle was a small one stowage space was very
severely restricted. All the examples which
were photographed seem to have carried all
manner of boxes, doubtless scrounged from the
usual sources, anywhere that they could be
fitted. Adding some of this excess stowage
always helps personalize a model by giving it
that touch of individuality. A 'jerrycan' rack
can also be made up from strip, and fitted.

Before painting the model can be dipped in a

solution of household detergent and allowed to dry. This removes any grease or mould-release agents which may remain on the parts.

The overall impression given by this kit is very good indeed. Resin kits call for a high level of patience and commitment if one wishes to get the best out of them and one must provide one's own markings but the end products are of excellent quality and well worth the effort and expense. However, it does pay to look around.

METAL KITS

There is still a great deal of prestige attached to metal military kits as these are closely related to the 'traditional' model soldiers. In the past, military vehicle kits have not really been taken seriously by the metal figure manufacturers. One concern that did keep

The very impressive completed model, well finished in an air-brushed tri-colour scheme with hand-painted markings. Model by David Parker.

faith with the metal kits, however, was John Piper models. His range of kits concentrate upon the First World War and are in the 'traditional' 1/32nd scale.

These kits cover all the troops and types of weapons used upon the Western Front during the conflict. Frequent additions are being made to the range.

Of most interest to the AFV modeller are the Rolls-Royce armoured car, the Renault FT and the Vickers 'Clyno' machine-gun carrier which only just qualifies as an armoured vehicle due to the sheet of armour plate fitted.

All three models are quite superb. For example, the Rolls-Royce AC consists of 164 castings in white metal and fifty-six etched

This is what you get in a metal kit: lots of parts and instructions.

brass components, all of the very highest quality. The spoked wheels are each made up from etched brass spoked sides, with white metal axles and tyres. The results are near perfection in scale, certainly the most realistic which can be obtained. An engine is supplied which adds to the potential of the vehicle in a scenic setting.

The Renault FT kit has more than 200 white metal parts and boasts a fully detailed interior and individual track links.

The 'Clyno' is to a similar standard, although it has fewer parts. It is one of my all-time favourites.

Fortunately, these models are obtainable from good model shops. A small specialist dealer may have a couple of kits in stock which you may be able to inspect.

There is, quite obviously, a price to pay for such high quality besides the cash one: they require a great deal of time and patience in order to make the most of them. Anyone can throw one together and make a mess of it!

WORKING METHOD

The parts are all carefully packed in separate sub-assembly bags. This is very handy as the best way to tackle the construction of one of these models is to make up the various sub-assemblies, then gradually join them up. The castings are usually flawless but each part is best checked and any traces of 'flash' or mould marks removed. The parts should then be trial-fitted together before being bonded. A little patience at this stage will prevent possible disasters later. When in doubt, trial-fit and work out where the part goes or how it relates to other parts and assemblies. If necessary, it is possible to hold assemblies together with Bluetack in order to work out exactly what goes where and how.

The best adhesive to use is quick-setting epoxy resin applied in the minimal quantities required to effect a good bond.

The parts may be clamped together or supported with Bluetack until the resin has set. The cyanoacrylate 'superglues' are strong, very fast setting, and convenient and are really essential for bonding etched brass parts. The 'jelly' type is rather easier to work with than the liquid, although the liquid seems to be more efficient. It is the ideal medium for assembling the whole kit but as it sets instantly there is little time for adjustment. It

also takes a long time to become familiar with its working properties, as the liquid seems to travel by capillary action to all sorts of places it should not. Most users suffer fingers glued together, parts glued to the knife, tweezers, modelling board, fingers etc. etc., during the apprenticeship and some modellers never seem to get the knack.

Although rather more difficult to assemble than plastic models there is nothing about the assembly of metal kits that is beyond the abilities of a fairly competent plastic modeller. Whilst the kits demand to be treated with respect they should not be held in awe. The end products will satisfy even the most critical modeller.

The Scale Link Rolls-Royce armoured car. This impressive model was built by Paul Williams.

VACUUM-FORMED MODELS

Another way in which manufacturers can offer a more specialist model is in the form of a sheet or sheets of vacuum-formed plastic. The parts are then cut out and assembled. In theory this is a rather easier process than scratch building but more difficult and involved than assembling a plastic kit. However, in my experience it is just about as easy to scratch build a model as it is successfully to make up a model of an armoured vehicle from one of these kits. The reason why this is so is that vacuum-formed models lack an essential crispness. This is the fault of the process rather than the designers. Forming the parts through the thickness of plastic sheet obviously reduces the sharpness. Reverse vacuum moulding, where the sheet is drawn *into* a mould, as opposed to *over* it,

promised better results but so far the process is not as acceptable for AFVs as it is for aircraft and 'B' vehicles. The latter are unarmoured or 'soft-skinned' vehicles, not intended to be directly exposed to fire, such as supply trucks. It is in the field of these 'B' vehicles, support types and so on that the process makes a realistic contribution. The rather softer aspect of these types is much more suitable for being depicted via this process. Even so, the models must be assembled with great care.

Working method
First of all, the parts must be cut from the sheet with great care. It is best to cut round

A fine example of a vacuum-formed model, built by Erik Johansen. Building one of these is akin to scratch building, with a little help from the kit.

them, then gently rub them over a sheet of abrasive paper until the edges are flat and square. The fit of the parts must be tested against each other at every stage of construction. Large areas are best reinforced with a medium thickness of sheet on the inner sides where it will not show. It is always best to secure the floor, chassis or base of the model to a flat surface, such as the modelling board, using twin-sided adhesive tape, to ensure that the model grows from a flat and true basis. The whole process is rather like an assisted means of scratch building. It does not have the real benefits of scratch building or those of the more usual form of kits.

Finally, the model must have its fine detail added from other sources. Items such as machine guns, steering wheels etc. must either be scrounged from other kits or be made up from scratch. To the experienced modeller, or perhaps to someone who cut his modelling teeth on model aircraft made by cutting out the parts from printed balsa sheet, building the 'skeleton', then covering it with fabric, models of this type present no real problems. To those used to the near perfection of current plastic kits, however, these items seem crude and difficult to make up. In the end, it all depends upon how much the model is wanted and upon how much effort one is willing to put into making it up.

In this chapter the various types of kits have been discussed. I hope the idea will have formed that no kit is perfect and that all can be improved to some extent. Also, I hope, the idea that some kits are beyond redemption will have been totally rejected. If one is willing to apply oneself and to tackle the problem, as opposed to sitting and thinking up reasons for not doing so, then it is possible to turn even a mediocre model into a true miniature of the real thing. Like anything else you improve with practice and, as one improves, so standards tend to rise. If you take the attitude that only the best that you can do is good enough then the modelling will give a great deal of pleasure, satisfaction and a very good end product. Making model kits to as high a standard as possible is the essential first stage of becoming a proficient modelmaker.

2 After Assembly

Once the model is assembled some modellers consider that the difficult part is only just starting. There is little doubt that painting and presenting the model in order to make it look a true miniature of the real thing requires at least the same amount of effort, patience and skill as the initial assembly.

Painting

The painted surface is the first thing to make an impact. A beautifully built model finished in a uninspired, plain finish will attract less favourable comment than a model of average quality realistically painted. In order to get the most out of the model it is essential to paint and present it as well as possible.

Many excellent modellers baulk at this stage. They seem to feel that their talents lie with the constructional aspect of the hobby and that the painting requires an artistic ability that one must be born with and which it is impossible to acquire. This sort of attitude is nonsensical! Anyone who is keen enough to learn constructional modelmaking skills can also learn to paint in a competent fashion. The trick is to be prepared to 'have a go'. Never approach the painting of a model in a hesitant fashion – find out the type of finished effect that pleases you most of all and go for it.

Again the modelling industry comes to the modeller's aid with a large range of paints, ways of applying them and visual references.

REFERENCES

Most box artwork gives a good idea of the finish appropriate to the vehicle type. The instructions contain alternative schemes. Japanese models are usually excellent in this respect. However, even the most poorly presented models contain some colour details. Just about the best general references it is possible to obtain are the famous Squadron/Signal publications. These days they tend to deal with a single vehicle type in great detail. They give a written history of the vehicle, scale drawings and, most importantly of all, comprehensive photographic coverage and fine colour artwork. The standard of research and accuracy is usually impeccable. The colour drawings show the schemes in an admirable fashion whilst the photographs show the overall appearance of the vehicles and the state that they usually got into on active service.

TOOLS FOR APPLYING PAINT

The modelmaker is very well served as regards paints. Modelling enamels are by far the most popular choice as they can easily be obtained in virtually any specific colour and are easy to apply. There are other types of paint but they have never really caught on and enamels will help 95 per cent of modellers achieve superb results 95 per cent of the time. Other paints do have their uses and they will be discussed as necessary.

There are two methods of applying the paint,

brushes and spray. The advice the writer would give is to find out what *you* are happy with and then buy the best materials you can.

Brushes

Some brushes are needed regardless: a good substantial one for applying general coats of paint, a flat one about 6 mm (¼ in.) wide for covering large areas and 'weathering', and a fine pointed one say size 2 or 3, for painting detail, lettering, markings and, of course, figures. Many modellers tend to use a very fine brush such as an 00 or even an 000 for painting detail. The logic behind their choice is impeccable: a finer brush allows one to paint finer detail – obvious isn't it? In point of fact, it is not quite that simple; a good size 3 will paint every bit as finely as an 00 and has the added bonus that it will carry enough paint to complete most smallish areas, unlike its tiny relatives. This brush should be of the very best quality that you can find; Kolinski sable is generally regarded as the best. Choose your own brush at an art or graphic shop and make sure that it 'points' well. The other brushes need not be of such very high quality, but do try to make sure that they are of sable; even an inferior sablebrush is better than any man-made substitute. Taking care of brushes is essential. Once painting is finished they should be rinsed in clean thinners then washed in soap and water. They should be carefully 'pointed' whilst still wet and always stored point upwards, in a jar or similar. By looking after your brushes it is quite possible to extend their useful lives by a factor or two or three.

Spraying

An ideal method of applying paint to models is with a miniature spray gun or an airbrush. Many modeller's spray guns are optimistically termed airbrushes by the manufacturers in an attempt to make them appear to be something that they very obviously are not. In fact the modeller's spray gun is probably more useful than the airbrush proper. With these items one can apply a smooth coat of paint very easily and quickly. To some extent one can localize the area of the spray in relation to the model but it is beyond the capabilities of a spray gun to reproduce camouflage patterns on a 1/35th scale model. To do this you really need a proper airbrush and these are rather expensive and temperamental items. They clog up very easily and are best used with thinned water-based paint of great covering power. Modeller's spray guns, on the other hand, will quite happily spray moderately thinned enamel and not clog up at the slightest excuse. If, however, you are keen on late wartime German armour with its spray-applied olive green and red brown over the base dark yellow, then there is no substitute for a decent airbrush. It takes some considerable practice to get the best out of one of these efforts but, as usual, the results are well worth the practice.

A decent modeller's spray gun costs about the same as a large Tamiya kit, whilst airbrushes *begin* at about six times this price. Fortunately there are compromises. Hybrid types exist and they can be best described as fine modeller's sprays or basic airbrushes. They can be adjusted to spray a jet which will cover a large area and are fine enough for a pattern of about 3 or 4 mm (1/10 in.) wide. Whilst they really are neither one thing or the other a very adequate performance can be coaxed out of them and they are highly recommended. They cost about half the price of a modest airbrush.

Providing the air power is another matter. Most modeller's spray guns come in a set with a hose and a can of propellant. This is fine if heavy use is not envisaged but the propellant always seems to run out on a Sunday when no shops are open and many individuals prefer a more reliable source of air pressure. A quite ingenious solution exists. There is an adaptor which fits onto a car tyre. The tyre is inflated and acts as a reservoir of compressed air; it will power the spray for some considerable time before it needs re-inflating. A suitable wheel may easily be had from a scrapyard and together with a foot pump it should cost no more than a couple of large kits. If you are really enthusiastic about spraying/airbrushing you should consider getting an electric motor. They are very expensive but also very reliable and convenient.

Many modeller's paints are formulated so that they may easily be sprayed/airbrushed; this is frequently at the expense of their application and covering power by brush. It is a good idea to find out which brands are best suited to spraying and never mix and match. A selection in the most used colours plus a few tints always come in useful. Most modelling enamels need to be thinned by about 10 to 15 per cent if they are to be sprayed from a modeller's spray gun in a pattern big enough to base-coat a 1/35th scale model; up to 25 per cent thinner should be added if a 'hybrid' type of gun is being used. High-quality airbrushes should not be risked with modeller's enamels. If a fine pattern is required then the enamel must be thinned even more and if a very fine pattern is essential then modeller's enamel should be discarded and a fine quality, water-based paint used instead. A perfect paint is artist's gouache. This is a very finely ground watercolour pigment and it combines strong colour with great covering power; even when highly thinned it covers well and it airbrushes beautifully. Its two main faults from the modeller's viewpoint are that it remains water-soluble and even after application it tends to fade with time. It is also very prone to damage from scuffing. A little liquid soap added to the solution helps it adhere and

improves its durability very much; protection from water and fading may be achieved by spraying with matt varnish. The best type of matt varnish is matt artist's fixative sold in spray cans and obtainable from any graphics supply shop. Apply this varnish in the finest possible mist coating and wait until it is completely dry before checking to see if it needs another, similar, coat to make it truly matt.

Once the model has been sprayed, left over paint should be emptied from the cup/jar, then thinners sprayed through, on the instrument's coarsest setting, until the spray jet is colourless. The instrument should then be stripped and cleaned before being reassembled. A drop of cellulose thinner sprayed through will confirm that the instrument is fully operational again and will remove any last vestiges of paint.

COLOUR

Now we come to the subject of colour itself. This is always one of the most controversial aspects of AFV modelling. Fortunately, most of the colours used are well published and quite well known although oddly enough the colours used by British forces in the Second World War still seem to generate some controversy. Be that as it may, it is not so much the colours themselves that are the problem, but how to depict them and how to represent patterns, weathering etc.

Even in peacetime when exact colours, patterns of application and marking standards are laid down there are variations. When British army vehicles were painted an overall dark, glossy green (the only 'proper' colour for military vehicles in my opinion) there were many variations in the colour. Most vehicles were a dark, 'cold' green, weathering to a blueish shade. Towards the end of the life of this colour scheme, prior to the introduction of the current matt green and black scheme, the shade of the paint changed to a much more brownish colour. If one saw a group of vehicles, of differing ages there did not seem to be a standard colour; all that one could say was that the general colour was dark, glossy green! This state of affairs existed in peacetime so it is quite easy to imagine the situation during prolonged hostilities.

Paint weathering and ageing must be taken into account, as it can change both the shade and the tone of the paint. For example, a newly issued factory fresh M4 Sherman would look rather different from a veteran of twelve months' active service in Italy. Not only would the new vehicle sport a pristine paint finish but it would carry all its markings and tactical signs correctly applied. On the veteran model, the dark olive drab paint would have weathered to a medium brownish-green with rust, grime, dust and fuel spillage much in evidence. In places the paint would be worn down to the metal and the large white stars which adorned the vehicle when new would probably have been painted out once the crew saw that anti-tank gunners used them as aiming marks. The olive drab used to paint out the stars would probably be a different shade to the original paint.

Matching paint to an exact specification or standard is a very difficult task, even under ideal conditions. In wartime many of the standard ingredients would not be available and substitutes would be used in their place. These would affect not only the basic coloration but also the covering power and resistance to fading.

It all sounds very complicated, but for-tunately most paint batches more or less matched up most of the time. It was, and still is, fairly obvious whether a vehicle is painted olive drab, dark green, dark earth or sand. Even the national differences are easily spotted once one knows a little about the subject. German desert sand, for example, was a rather darker and richer shade than the colour used by the British army.

But, as is nearly always the case, there is another factor to complicate matters. If a model were to be painted in exactly the correct colour then it would look far too dark. The scale model must be painted with scale paint, a fact long recognized by model railway enthusiasts. This is because large surfaces reflect back a great deal of light, and because the real vehicles live outdoors whilst the models are usually viewed indoors in artificial light. Fortunately the paintmakers are aware of the problem and have toned down their paints in an appropriate manner. Colour artwork usually shows the correct scale effect and may be relied upon, most of the time, as a guide.

Once one has researched the subject, bought the paint and decided upon the colour scheme to be employed, all is ready – or is it? There are further decisions to be made: is the vehicle to depict a new example or is it to look as if it is a faded veteran? Will it be weathered and if so lightly or heavily? If the model is to depict a new machine, many AFV modellers prefer a 'museum' collection of vehicles as they *should* have appeared whilst others, myself included, prefer their models to look used, in fact very well used. In between both of these extremes lies the middle ground where the effect to please most modellers may be found. It should be noted, however, that AFVs really do get themselves into some very dirty states indeed, especially if they are tracked. As they spend much of their active lives ploughing through mud or on roads rapidly breaking up under their weight and are never washed when under fire, it is really little wonder.

To some extent the condition of the finished model has an influence upon the initial cost. If the vehicle is to be depicted in 'ideal' condition, then it is best to choose a lighter shade of the appropriate colour. If it is felt that the colour looks a little too dark fresh from the tin then it should be lightened. A little yellow can be added to olive drab, sand to dark green or dark earth and white to sand or dark yellow. If the vehicle is to be extensively weathered on the other hand, then it is best to use the correct tone, or, ideally, a very slightly richer and darker one. This is so that the base colour will glow through the weathering and not be lost under it. Models which lose their base colour always seem to look a little scruffy and somehow uncompleted. Most modellers want the vehicle to look attractive, to some extent idealized and 'vital' – and this is not the same as being drably accurate.

PAINTING TECHNIQUES

The base coat

When applying the base coat, either by brush or by spray, make sure that the model is given a coat thin enough not to obscure fine detail. If problems exist with the covering power of the thinned down paint, work on the theory that two thin coats are a lot better than one thick one. When applying the second coat, allow the first one to dry out for at least twelve hours. In my experience this is where the spray unit pays for itself as it is evident that if the first coat is applied by brush it seems to have a solvent effect on the adhesive, and all sorts of small and seemingly firmly attached parts come adrift. Some areas also seem to get missed! It does not seem to be strictly necessary either to degrease or to undercoat the model before applying the base coat even when working with metal models; the covering power of modern enamels is excellent and the solvents seem to dispose of any surface grease.

Overpainting

Once the initial coat is on the overpainting, if any, may be considered. The base coat should be allowed about twenty-four hours to dry out. There are three types of overpainting on the real vehicles, which should be considered when modelling. The first is 'hard edged', where the colour has been applied by brush in well-defined areas: typically, this might be used for the British tri-colour desert scheme of the early war period. The second type is 'soft edged', where colour is oversprayed in a fairly random manner as for the famous German-three colour pattern. Finally, there is the 'overpainted' look, where a standard base colour is overpainted with another so it may blend in better with new surroundings or conditions. Examples are white overpainting to blend in with winter conditions or sand to blend in with the desert.

The 'hard edged' type is quite simple to apply with a brush. It is best to define the areas to be painted *very lightly* with a soft pencil prior to painting. If the colour to be overpainted is similar in tone to the base coat it is a good idea to make it either richer, lighter or darker so as to emphasize their differences with rather more contrast than would be the case in reality. In real life much of this overpainting was applied in an inconsistent manner and brush marks and differing densities of paint were very apparent. Frequently the base coat showed through. It is best not to overdo this type of sloppy effect – often the model simply looks badly painted – however, if quite thin paint is used the effect is given in an acceptable manner. A close study of wartime photographs shows that the German overpainting was definitely not always carried out with a spray gun and was, in fact, very crudely applied. Reproducing this effect in model scale never looks quite right, and the best effects are achieved if the model is finished in an 'artistic' manner.

Back to the famous German three-colour scheme. As German tanks are, by far the most widely modelled types, this colour scheme is probably the one most frequently applied. By mid '42 German combat vehicles in Europe and Russia were painted in a base coat of dark yellow. Tins of olive green and red brown were supplied; they could be thinned with either petrol or water and were supposed to be applied, with a spray gun, by the crew so as to blend the vehicle into the local landscape. The spray gun seems to have been the first item of equipment lost but even if it was retained a lot depended upon the artistic skill of the crew member selected to do the spraying, the amount and kind of thinner added to the paint and the whims of the unit commander. Evidently if the paint was thinned with water it did not last very long; it appears that even a heavy dew could cause it to run. Under 'ideal' conditions, i.e. behind the lines during a period of rest, re-equipping or retaining, the colour schemes would be carefully applied and this is when the vehicles would probably be most photographed. Be that as it may, this is a scheme most AFV modellers find attractive and want to reproduce. As always, practice makes perfect. Prior to 'attacking' the model, spray a decent-sized piece of sheet with the dark yellow base colour. Artist's gouache should be thinned until it sprays easily then the airbrush 'tuned' until the desired width of spray jet is achieved. This paint will adhere to the base coat much better if a little liquid soap is added to the mix. Practise spraying upon the sheet until the best effect is obtained. When it is time to spray the model it is a very good idea to 'draw' the pattern on the model using very thin lines of diluted colour, simply follow these lines with the airbrush. Once the scheme is applied allow it to dry out completely, then protect it with a thin coat of matt varnish.

That is the best way to do it in theory. However, sometimes it seems a little too subtle and the paint seems to get lost under weathering. I prefer a much bolder approach using a piece of equipment rather less sophisticated than the airbrush. When your best brush is showing signs of deterioration it can be used as a 'dry brush'. Cut off the end to eliminate the point and it is ready to go. Load the brush with paint, then wipe off most of it with a tissue. Trail the brush over paper until it is leaving a faint, broken line then apply the overpainting pattern using a light, tightly circular, 'scrubbing' motion. The effect is excellent as the paint feathers towards the edge and is denser and darker in the centre, as is the real thing. This method of applying the scheme gives more definition and contrast.

Finally the hastily applied, extemporized schemes must be considered. These included whitewash applied when the snows came, and mud applied to Panzer grey vehicles in the desert early on in that campaign and to the olive drab American vehicles at the end of it. It is pointless to paint the vehicle overall in, say, mud colour as the base colour always showed through the extemporized mud coating which served as camouflage. It is quite a difficult task to try to reproduce paint like this and keep the model looking attractive, but it can be done and done in some style. A fine sand finish may be had by setting the spray/airbrush to its fine setting so that it gives a pattern about 12 mm (½ in.) wide, then painting over the model in swift, long strokes. If a 'swirling' motion is used an equally good effect is obtained. The same method can be used to obtain a whitewashed affect, but a much nicer one may be had with a brush. Thin down the white and cover about half of the area of the model using short, irregularly applied strokes. Thin down the paint some more, then fill in the other areas; do not worry about covering the previously applied white – this simply gives a denser-looking white. Finally, scrub over any remaining gaps using a dry brush and a very thin white. To obtain a faded effect, use the paint well thinned down from the start so that the base coat shows through rather strongly.

Tools and tyres

Once the basic finish has been applied, the road wheel tyres should be painted. Tyres are not black; they are at best dark grey and usually a sort of brownish grey. It is not difficult to depict this colour but tonally it is frequently very similar to olive drab, dark green and Panzer grey. Try to make the colour a little darker in tone than the base coat. It always helps to emphasize a difference.

Tools are not the same colour as the tank; they would certainly have been removed if the vehicle was overpainted, then replaced. Usually tools are finished off in a semi-matt drab finish, generally green. This is very much more durable than matt paint. Wooden parts are also usually painted although nobody would object to natural wood finish. Strapping is invariably a drab webbing. A nice semi-gloss finish may be had by painting the tools in matt paint, then coating them in silk-finish varnish. The same applies to machine gun barrels, which can be painted matt black and then varnished.

MARKINGS

Finally, markings must be considered be they national, unit or tactical. Transfers/decals are usually supplied with a kit and most of them are of a very high standard. Some others are available sold as separate sheets but there are not as many as there used to be. Some can be obtained in the form of rub-down sheets. Applying transfers has always been considered a bit of a headache by the modelling fraternity. They must usually be applied over some detail parts such as vision flaps, rivets or grab handles. Their finish is usually semi-gloss and therefore different from the finish of the model.

Finally, the covering varnish always shows a thin extension of the decal. Rub-down markings seem to be the perfect answer but they are rather more difficult to apply and tend to break up whilst being put on. There is no doubt, however, that if one is willing to persevere with this type of marking and to become skilled in its application, that they do give exceedingly good results. The main snag is that they are available in a very limited range. So it is back to good old decals. One idea currently in favour with aircraft modellers is to paint the model in gloss finish to which the decals adhere perfectly, 'pulling' themselves in to panel lines etc. The model is then matt varnished. This seems fine for model aircraft but not really robust enough looking for AFVs. A variation of this theme can, however, be used on our models with greater success. It demands care in application, attention to detail and a good deal more effort than simply sticking the transfers to the model, but the end results are impressive.

Remove the required parts from the decal sheet, then trim away the varnish from them as closely as you can. Obviously this is easier with large, simple shapes such as stars or crosses than it is with serial numbers. A coat of clear liquid floor polish is now applied to the areas where the decals are to be applied. It is best to coat the whole panel or area as there might be a slight variation in colour which would otherwise be noticeable. When dry apply the decals, positioning them carefully and blotting them with a tissue. Apply another thin coat of polish and allow to dry out completely. Finish off with the thinnest possible coat of matt varnish which will still give a matt surface. If done properly this looks as if the decals have been painted on.

Of course, painting on the markings is the perfect solution. Just like the real thing. Needless to say, it is also the process which requires the greatest skill. Of course many markings were roughly applied, as is obvious from any study of photographs, but most units seem to have had a signwriter who was a valuable member of the team. This is very

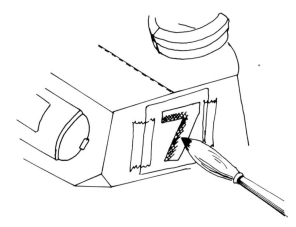

To apply lettering, cut a stencil from cartridge paper and dab in the letter using thick paint.

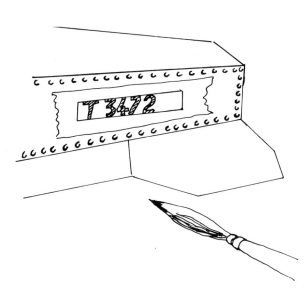

When small lettering is required, cut a window out of adhesive tape and use as a guide.

evident if one looks at photographs of British and American vehicles. As usual there are ways round this problem. In real life most markings were applied with the aid of stencils and it is an easy process to make up your own.

Apply the markings or large-letter decal to a sheet of stiff paper then, when dry, cut it out. There is your stencil! If the stencil is held in the relevant position then the marking may be applied by dabbing through thickish paint using a medium brush. Once the marking is painted on it can be cleaned up quite easily using thinned paint and a fine brush. This is a very useful method of applying national and tactical markings; unfortunately it is no use whatsoever for smaller serial numbers of the type, for example, carried by Allied vehicles during the war. It is possible to letter them in neatly by hand but some people never seem to be able to get the knack of doing this. If a rectangle is cut out of adhesive tape the overall size of the lettering block and then applied to the vehicle, the hole acts as a guide preventing the lettering from running astray, which is the main problem most modellers have with hand lettering. Other than that one may purchase a sheet of very small rub-down letters from graphic suppliers and apply them.

Exhausts, where visible, are best painted in a combination of grey and rust; if the rust looks somewhat garish it may be toned down with a thin wash of matt black.

Tracks are always a problem – getting them right, making them hang correctly and, in this instance, painting them up to look realistic. It is best to paint the tracks off the vehicle and to wrap them round a piece of thick card; when one side is painted the tracks can be turned and the other side tackled. The metallic colour in which most of them are moulded is a good base colour. Most tracks took a real hammering and very quickly became rusty and dirty. A good overall basis for this colour is one part rust paint (all ranges include one) added to the same amount of earth with a hint of black added to tone down the mix. A thin wash of black tones it down even further and helps define the detail. This wash should ideally be thinners tinted with matt black, several thin washes being far preferable to one thick coat.

The raised parts of the track may then be highlighted with a 'gunmetal' mix made by

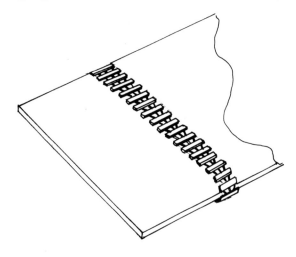

Fit tracks round a piece of cardboard as shown, so that they can be easily painted.

adding matt black to silver. If the paint is quite thick, i.e. unthinned, and then most of it is wiped off the loaded brush the brush can then be lightly dragged across the surface. The paint will 'catch' exactly where it is supposed to and give an effective finished result. Next a little more silver should be added to the paint, the brush loaded and wiped very nearly dry. When it is scrubbed over a sheet of paper it should leave just a trace of colour behind. Flick over the track surface with this mix, add some more silver and repeat. The track surface should look as if made from weathered metal rubbed away to bright upon its bearing surfaces. Once dry (allow at the very least twenty-four hours), the

tracks can be removed from the card, twisted inside out, replaced on the card then the inner surface painted. Where the rubber tyres come into contact the metal is usually polished bright, and good silver paint gives a fine effect. If the track has central guide horns then they will usually be quite clean and well polished but if the track is fitted with outer ones only the inside will be in this condition. The other parts of the track should be painted as for the outside except that the 'rust' may be allowed to be a little more lurid.

Once the tracks are fitted the model is painted as an example of the vehicle in prime condition. Many modellers leave things at this stage. Others consider the model to be at a basic stage in this form and want to depict the AFV as it might have appeared on active service. They want the crew's personal effects and the crew figures added, the model weathered, and finally the model presented upon a scenic base. It is these processes that we will examine next.

Stowage

One of the perennial problems with AFVs is that there never seems to be enough room to hold all the crew's effects, spare fuel and so on. Photographs, especially of American, British and German vehicles, show that they are usually covered with a plethora of bundles, boxes and cans. All of these were decidedly non-standard fitments; the bundles contained bedding, the boxes rations, clothing, cooking gear etc. and the cans petrol, oil and water. Other items 'liberated' from the enemy were frequently carried. Many of them indeed were greatly prized and considered superior to issue pieces, the prime example being the famous 'jerry cans'. These were German five-gallon fuel/water containers which were a vast improvement on the British flimsy cans which split and leaked at the slightest provocation. Items such as national flags and recognition panels were also frequently carried on the turret top or rear decking to identify the vehicle's nationality from the air to friendly aircraft.

How much of this is represented on models is a matter of personal choice. As remarked previously, many modellers like to depict their vehicles as standard issue and finish and battened down. However there is little doubt that some stowage helps the model look more like a miniature of the real thing.

It is now possible to buy kits or packs of accessories for the purpose of 'stowing up' a model vehicle. These items are normally very good indeed, especially the boxes, crates, packs, fuel cans, camouflage nets etc. 'Bundles' representing rolled-up bedding always look as if they are moulded in plastic. These are best made from tissue rolled up, tied with thread and finished off with paper straps; a tiny piece of card depicts the buckle quite well. They are soaked in a thin solution of white glue and water, then moulded to the vehicle so that they look as if they belong there. Boxes made from planks are also very easily represented by scribed sheet. The great advantage of making up one's own boxes is that they may be made to measure for the particular model.

All these items need be secured to the model as on the real thing although ammunition boxes were frequently welded to American and British vehicles as a matter of course. Bundles and boxes ought to be tied or strapped down with paper 'strapping' or thread 'ropes'. Packs should have straps fitted to them to make it look as if they really are secured to the vehicle. Very few things look worse on a model than extra stowage seemingly defying the laws of gravity. It is essential to take care in positioning these items so that they will not evidently foul the vehicle's weaponry or prevent access to filler caps, radiator etc.

It is always a good idea to paint the stowage before adding it to the model. In the case of tissue 'bundles', if some watercolour is added to the white-glue solution then the piece may be dyed at the same time as it is fixed.

Weathering

Armoured vehicles get very dirty on active service. Added to the normal filth that covers them rapidly during peacetime manoeuvres are the signs of wear, tear, neglect and damage.

How much of this is to be depicted is up to the individual as is, to some extent, the style of the weathering. Some modellers prefer a fairly gentle effect whilst others, myself included, like the vehicles to look as if they have been through a mud bath!

Most modellers see a style applied to a model that attracts them and use this as a basis for their weathering efforts. A visit to a modelling club meeting is usually all that is needed to inspire those who want to weather their models but are a little uncertain as to how. If you want to see the effects of intimate contact between the environment and large powerful vehicles, then you need only visit a major construction site. Looking at large contractors' vehicles ploughing through the mud will very quickly show you the state to which vehicles are reduced on service. Take notes and better still, reference photographs.

After a few models most of us tend to develop a quite distinct style of weathering. However, one really needs to develop a number of styles to suit both the colour scheme of the vehicle and the condition of the environment in which it is envisaged as operating. Heavy weathering suits vehicles finished in plain dark colours most of all. Complex camouflage paint schemes seem to

David Parker's subtly finished T34/85 shows a rather more artistic style of weathering.

get lost under really heavy weathering, as do desert or winter finishes. If the model is 'wearing' decals/transfers, the edges always show through heavy weathering of this nature in a most embarrassing fashion no matter how carefully they have been applied.

The factors to consider are:

A   The age and general condition of the vehicle. Is it an old, battered veteran or a newly issued vehicle?

B   Is it operating in an urban or open country environment?

C   What are the weather conditions prevailing at the time? In wet weather the vehicles will be muddy if operating in rough country or wallowing along muddy tracks which are rapidly breaking down. If they are engaged in a street fight during rain, where the top half also gets covered with soot and ash from burning buildings, they will simply be dripping with filth. On the other hand, if there has been a long, settled spell of fine weather then the vehicles will probably be very dusty indeed. Always take this particular factor into account, especially if the model is to be displayed upon a scenic base.

D   Will the camouflage scheme be lost under extensive weathering?

E   Artistic licence.

Having taken all these factors into account, it is time to make a start on painting the weathering on to the model. The ideal brush for weathering models is a flat one between 7 and 14 mm (¼–½ in.) wide. Sable hair is best of all. A spray unit is useful for adding coats of dust.

WEAR AND TEAR

Any wear and tear effects should be applied first. The crew clambering over the vehicle are bound to wear away the paint. Even the most cursory inspection of a vehicle in service will show that the paint wears away about the ingress areas. It is also liable to wear away about the wheel rims, drive sprocket teeth, and indeed anywhere the vehicle has been in prolonged contact with the environment. In the most used areas the paint will have been worn down to bare metal. In others the primer will be exposed and in the case of overpainted vehicles the base colour will show through. As an example a Panther operating in Normandy after D Day would frequently have been driving across country where the road wheels would have been polished by the tall grass. It would have constantly been brushed by foliage in the narrow bocage lanes and much of the overpainting would have been worn away, especially on the hard edges. On the model the overpainting may simply be scraped away using the edge of a blade. Bare metal is best depicted by highlighting hard edges and raised detail with silver paint to which a hint of grey has been added.

RUST, FUEL SPILLAGE AND DUST

Rust always appears wherever it can. If a vehicle bumps into a wall (usually with fatal consequences for the wall) and a good deal of paint is removed exposing bare metal then, sure enough, next morning it will be sporting a fine layer of red rust. Even tracks develop a bright red coating after a night's inactivity. Chief victims of rust are usually sheet metal fittings, locks, trackguard supports and so on; these are made of a lower quality metal and are more prone to rusting than thick, high-quality steel. Rust also seems to accumulate about rivets and then run down from them following a bout of rain. Rain also inevitably washes out rust from its hidden breeding grounds into rather more visible areas. Anyone who has kept a car for more than about five years will know exactly what I mean! Red rust always looks 'over the top' on a model no matter how realistic it may, in fact, be. It is best to depict rust as a dullish red-brown. Adding a little earth paint to rust colour helps no end. A good method of depicting rust is very carefully to paint in the parts with the dull rust colour then dry-brush, very lightly, with the 'pure' rust colour. It is best to use the fine brush at this stage and to wipe off most of the rust once it has been loaded; there should be just enough colour left on the brush to leave the faintest trace when it is 'worked' over the relevant area. Two or three applications are always better than one thick, clumsy application. Fuel spillage is usually a greyish trail of discoloration in the case of petrol whilst diesel is a distinct rather shiny black. Thinned drawing ink depicts spilled diesel beautifully.

There is always a temptation to overdo these effects. Once one begins to enjoy the process and sees the results there is a tendency to keep on going and spoil things. It is always best to pre-plan the effects desired then stick to them. When in doubt stand back and look, think about it. A little less is nearly always better than too much. The reverse side of the coin is that many people underdo these effects so that they are hardly noticeable. They are best regarded as part of the overall finish and should be distinctive but not overpowering.

Applying the final coating is not nearly so difficult as it sounds. Indeed, a coating of dust is quite a simple matter. Begin by mixing up an earth colour to which a little sand and white has been added; the effect should be rather subdued and drab. Lightly overspray the whole of the chassis pan and suspension and give the front an extra coat. It should only be a very light coat and the base colour *must* be clearly visible through it. As has been made apparent so often, several very thin coats are *always* much better than one which is too thick. One thick coat of paint simply acts as another base coat and changes the basic colour scheme. Add some more sand and white to the mix and lightly overspray the model from a fair distance. Again allow for a slightly heavier build-up from the front. If the dust is to be shown, for example, as scuffed by the crew's movements or by foliage then mark the wet coating with a stiff brush. This is simple and effective. As an alternative to applying the overall coating, it is possible to dust the model with either jeweller's rouge, a grinding paste used in lapidary and obtainable from most craft shops, or the relevant shade of face powder. Applied with a large soft brush it adheres very well indeed and gives a most realistic, if not fully permanent, effect.

HEAVY WEATHERING EFFECTS

As mentioned before, the heavier weathering effects seem to suit only models which have a plain finish. When a finish of this nature is applied over a complex colour scheme it usually looks simply messy and loses the carefully applied colour scheme.

A decent depiction of mud may be had by mixing earth paint with talcum powder and spreading it about the chassis and running gear with an old and soft brush. As it is drying out it can be worked with a stiff brush to give it a little more texture. If a 'mud and grass' effect, so often found when vehicles are moving across country, is required, then mix in a little fibre-type grass scenic dressing – made from pre-dyed sawdust, flock or fibres – with the paint and powder 'mud'.

When it is fully dried this 'mud' may be chipped away from the wheels, suspension etc. in the way that dried mud would come away in real life. It can simply be scraped or prised off with the craft knife. If, on the other hand, the mud is to be shown as fresh then a coat of matt or silk varnish gives the desired effect to perfection. 'Mud' may be applied over 'normal' weathering or be used as the basis of it.

Dry brushing
Whether or not mud is applied, the heaviest weathering is always around the chassis pan/running gear; usually an earth colour lightened with a dry brush but as this term covers a multitude of effects perhaps a detailed description of both the term and practice may be in order. Dry-brushing, as the term implies, is a method of applying a minute trace of paint to give a feathered effect and incomplete coverage. The amount of paint applied and the degree of feathering depends upon the amount of paint left on the brush. If a brush loaded with paint is trailed along a sheet of paper, the line that it paints will be smooth and complete at first. As the paint is expended and the brush begins to dry out the line will become fainter and tend to feather, especially at the edges. As the brush continues to dry out the line grows progressively fainter and more feathered until it leaves just the faintest trace of colour before disappearing completely. The term 'dry brushing' covers all the stages between the feathering first appearing and the pigment leaving only the faintest of traces.

The initial coating is best applied by loading the brush with colour, then wiping most of it away with a tissue. The brush is then lightly scrubbed over a sheet of paper until it begins to stop covering completely and begins to feather. It is helpful if the paint is unthinned, as thick paint always dry brushes better. The paint may then be, quite boldly, scrubbed over the sides of the chassis and running gear. The model's nose and rear plates should have this coat applied using short vertical strokes, starting at the bottom and trailing away towards the top of the stroke. Boldness at this stage pays dividends.

Some white is then added to the paint, enough to lighten it noticeably and make it look 'chalky'. The brush is loaded, wiped, then scrubbed until the coverage is faint and the feathering distinctive. Extend this coating all over the sides of the vehicle, using brush strokes as opposed to a scrubbing motion. Vertical strokes are fine for the front and rear plates but the sides should be treated with strokes at a distinct angle – about 45 degrees is ideal. This makes the vehicle look as though it became weathered whilst travelling at speed. If the strokes are kept light then the paint will first of all give the kind of coverage intended and secondly hit any raised detail, helping it stand out.

More white should be added to the mix and, if it is starting to look a little too chalky, a little yellow can be used. The brush is then loaded, wiped and scrubbed until only the faintest trace of pigment is evident. This is applied overall to the model with light, 'slapping' strokes following the general direction of the previous strokes. This coat is especially effective as it tends to hit only the raised detail, highlighting it against the rather darker base colour and weathering. It also defines texture and hard edges as well as generally making the model look realistic. Some modellers will always go for a restrained version of this finish but I must confess to greatly preferring a 'full-blooded' approach,

resulting in an almost impressionistic look.

Between the two suitable weathering effects will be found for all models in all situations; parade-ground finishes are simply well painted models minus the weathering.

Once the weathering is applied it is an excellent idea to give the model a thin wash of matt black. The black runs into the panel lines and defines them in a positive and most convincing way and it also tones down the weathering. It is best to use black drawing ink added to water; test it by brushing over white paper, which it should tint light grey; brush on evenly and it will dry nicely matt. Give the model a fine, even wash and mop up any pools where they tend to collect. When dry, check whether the desired effect has been achieved and apply further coats until it has. Care and restraint are needed if the effect is not to be overdone.

It has only been possible to give a general description of weathering. Every modeller eventually modifies the techniques to give a distinctive style. Painting styles are now coming back to a more realistic 'warts and all' style after being dominated for nearly a decade by the 'glowing oils' school which produced very pretty but hardly realistic tank models. There is little doubt, however, that weathering, if carefully applied with the added flair given by a little artistic licence, enhances the finished appearance of any model.

Crew figures

If we accept that extra stowage and weathering enhance a model's appearance by adding an extra dimension of realism, then it is fairly obvious that a miniature vehicle crew, or part of a crew, will add greatly to the overall effect.

A few years ago AFV crew figures were very poor. Some were simply bad, being incorrectly proportioned and wrongly uniformed. The first specific products which came from the Orient looked, at first, very good indeed. Unfortunately, the stature of the figures was that of typical Japanese males with European features grafted on. They never looked quite right no matter how well they were painted. The first plastic items from Italeri were no better; whilst they were fairly well proportioned they were very stiff and perhaps their arms and fingers were rather too finely drawn.

Of late things have greatly improved. It is now largely possible to buy the crews from the various kits as separately packaged sets, which saves a good deal of money. The best news of all, however, is that the supporting industry has turned its hand to supplying the missing items and the quality ranges from the very good to the spectacular. Belgo, Hornet and Piper model figures are all excellent, full of character and, best of all, to scale. Other models made by different concerns are equally good and, again, are coming on to the market all the time. Verlinden figures are second to none as regards quality. However they are true 54 mm figures and would, in 1/35th scale, work out at about two metres (6ft 4in.). Latest releases are somewhat smaller but they are still big lads. Fortunately, larger figures, providing that the vehicle is quite a large machine, manage to look right, whereas ones that are too small never do. It is readily apparent that people come in all shapes and sizes, but this does not really work in model form. Unless one is aiming at a 'personality', then figures of differing statures look uneasy. Perhaps, as in painting and weathering effects, too much realism simply does not look attractive or idealized enough. As most of us want our models to look perfect we always aim for an attractive appearance. Incidentally it is worth pointing out that too many big fellows tend to overwhelm all but the largest models.

I have mixed feelings about these first-rate releases. Whilst they are smashing models that are eagerly ordered and bought they are eroding hard-won skills in converting figures to particular styles from the most unlikely sources. When these figures were not available, military modellers had to learn the whys and wherefores of converting figures to different types of uniforms and re-animating them to new configurations. I well remember scrounging historical model figures given away with a French breakfast cereal. Five of these were turned into a prize-winning group of mechanized troops and another, given away to a friend, won first prize in the single-figures category at the following year's show. If for example, you wanted French troops, then you needed to find suitable-sized figures, strip them down to the right configuration and then build up the trousers from modelling putty, add the puttees and greatcoat from paper before building up the webbing and personal equipment from plastic, paper and putty. The helmets could be rubbed and cut down from more readily available types. In practice, you spent as much time on the figures as on scratch-building a model.

These days most types are available, the more popular German and American ones in a bewildering variety. The only real skill that need be acquired is the ability to re-animate the figures so that they conform to one's own ideas of the intended relationship with the vehicle.

There is still plenty of scope for modellers who wish to produce unusual figures but a description of the practice of modifying and converting figures is well outside of the scope of this book; besides this there are plenty of first class works on the subject which are readily available.

Most AFV modellers tend to regard the figures as accessories to the vehicles. Unless the care that is lavished upon the models of the

This Belgo crewman by David Parker looks nearly real.

The long and short of it: one of the largest World War II vehicles, the King Tiger (David Parker), compared with one of the smallest, the Renault UE (Alan Ranger).

David Parker's tank crew features figures extensively converted from other sources.

vehicles is applied to the figures, however, the overall effect will be spoilt and the model would look better without figures at all.

A few ideas on figures are shown in the photographs. There is really very little difficulty involved in animating and modifying figures. With a little practice, the skills can be acquired by any competent modeller. It is the painting that tends to cause the problems.

PAINTING FIGURES

Many vehicle modellers tend to be rather chary of figure painting simply because they lack confidence in their own abilities. They need have nothing to fear. First of all, the uniforms worn are generally practical and drab and require nothing like the skill involved in painting the complex uniforms of, say, the late eighteenth or early nineteenth centuries. Painting the features seems to cause most problems. In fact nearly all modellers can teach themselves to make a competent, if not inspired, job of painting model figures. The secret is to evolve a simple method which can be improved upon as one acquires the relevant skills.

A good basis for feature painting is to buy a proprietary brand of flesh colour. If it looks a little pallid when applied, add a little reddish brown to it and check it against the back of the hand to see if it matches. This is a good way of checking out the colour, but more importantly, the tone of the mix, as there is always a tendency to make flesh colours too light. Once a successful colour is found, or mixed, put it to one side and only use it for figures no matter how useful it may seem for other jobs. You will then need a shading and a highlighting colour. In practice the best shading colour is a fairly deep reddish brown. It should be much more brown than red of course. The highlighting is provided, simply enough, by white.

Before painting make sure the figures sport no gaps or mould marks. Undercoat the figures in white and allow to dry thoroughly. Paint in the eye sockets, around the nose, under the lip and chin and the centre of the ears in the shading colour. Paint the rest of the head with flesh, then add an equal amount of white to a little flesh and highlight the bridge of the nose, the cheekbones, the jaw line and the chin. The lips are best painted in a mix of flesh, shading colour and deep red. A little of this mix added to the flesh can be applied to give some colour to the cheeks. In all this is a very simple but effective way of painting facial features. It looks good, helps them stand out and can be used as the basis of a developing style.

It is best to paint clothing in an overall dark shade, then overpaint all except the recesses of the creases in a lighter shade and finally highlight with an even lighter shade. Pockets, seams, overlaps and so on are best delineated with very thin lines of the basic colour darkened as far as possible.

All of these suggestions are, of necessity, rather basic. They are only intended to get started modellers who may have little confidence in their skills in this area. As confidence grows so will ability, and a clear individual style will emerge.

If one accepts that the figures must look natural, that they should complement the vehicle and that the same amount of care should be lavished upon them as upon the main model then you will not go far wrong.

Final presentation

If a vast amount of effort has been expended upon making the model, stowing, weathering and crewing it, then it seems to be rather a shame not to present it within the confines of its own miniature environment.

Displaying the model on a scenic base serves two purposes. First of all it enhances the model's appearance by setting it off against its natural habitat. Secondly, it protects the model by ensuring that the base and not the model is handled.

As with model soldiers, there are books on the market dealing in most comprehensive fashion with this matter and it would not be in keeping with the aims of the book to describe fully this aspect of modelling. The best books upon the topic of scenic modelling are those written as a guide to railway modellers.

As is so often the case, the supporting cottage industry is making available everything, or just about everything, needed in this sphere of modelmaking. It is possible to buy large and small ruined structures, roadways, natural groundwork, signposts, animals, rubble, clutter etc. Most of these are very very good indeed. In a matter of hours it is possible to create a scenic base which would once have taken a week of modelling. This is the way the hobby is going. About the only scenic artefacts that are not available to an acceptable standard are trees and, doubtless, they are on their way.

SCENIC BASES

Scenic bases can be as simple or as complicated as you like. The simplest one is a depiction of a piece of groundwork just a little larger than the model.

It is best to use a piece of blockboard for the base in order that it may be as strong and firm as possible. Most timber shops will sell offcuts at a very reasonable price and half a dozen pieces of various sizes will mount a year's modelling projects. The baseboard should be scored heavily with a knife so that the scenic modelling medium, usually plaster, will grip. The plaster is then mixed, spread over the board and modelled roughly to shape using a damp sponge. As an alternative, thin-sheet expanded polystyrene may be used and sanded to the relevant contours. It can then be dressed with a thin skin of plaster. If more texture is desired then bran or sawdust may be added to the plaster. Use fabric dyes or food colouring to dye the plaster to an appropriate colour. It is best to press tank tracks into the groundwork whilst it is still wet. It is a good idea to have a couple of spare sets to press firmly into the plaster; when they are removed from the dry plaster they leave very realistic tracks. It is always important to remember to do this. It looks totally wrong if the tank is in the middle of a field and there is no indication as to how it arrived there.

The ground may then be dressed with scenic dressing reinforced with a few clumps of longer 'grass' made by planting clumps of sisal string into the wet plaster. In order to ensure that the scenic dressing stays in position, it may be lightly oversprayed with a white-glue solution. A simple plant spray is the ideal appliance for this process. Most painting will be carried out using the modelling spray. Thin washes of colour help build up a subtle effect.

ROADWAY

Roadway is similarly modelled, except that it is rather simpler as it is smoother. A good depiction of earth tracks/roads may be had by gluing down fish-tank gravel over the road area. When dry it should be covered with a minimal skim of plaster. Much of this plaster can then be 'stroked' away with a damp sponge so that many of the 'stones' surface. This gives a good depiction of roads made by beating earth over a rubble core which were common, until quite recently, in rural Europe. Drainage ditches should line the roads and they are usually shown as rank with grass and reeds.

A smooth plaster surface is easily scribed to represent cobblestones and rubble is very nicely shown using cat litter dusted with a mix of cigarette ash and plaster powder. Ruined chunks of building may be added, directly from the box, to this sort of base and then painted once in situ.

TREES

Trees are always a problem. Those damaged in the course of battle are fortunately quite simple to depict well. Most domestic heathers and rose trees have very complex roots which, when washed, look great as shattered parts of trees. Simply tear them apart and scatter them about. Trunks themselves may be had by using a piece of twig of about finger thickness scored, if necessary, to give the effect of rough bark. Make sure it is planted firmly and that the top is very obviously snapped as opposed to clipped or sawn through.

Full-sized trees can very often be depicted by heathers bought from any ga en centre and pampas grass can be turned into an excellent scale Lombardy poplar with very little effort. The basis of a tree may be had from privet clippings, a suitable piece being 'branched out' with teased-out wire wool and then dressed with the dried sawdust type of scenic dressing.

All this is very rudimentary stuff. It should serve, however, to start you off on the right footing. After you have learned to apply the rudiments in a practical and satisfactory manner, then the more advanced aspects seem to come naturally. Finally, most bases look best if nicely finished off. Rough edges can be sanded smooth and painted or, better still, covered with wood veneer or plastic sheet. Remember that any effort expended in presentation is always worthwhile.

3 Converting Models

When a vehicle is accepted for service it is normally somewhat different from its prototype; experience and a rapidly changing specification ensure that. At the end of a long service life the final version seems even further removed from the original concept. In some extreme instances every part of the vehicle will have been altered. Improvements will have been made to firepower, protection, automotive efficiency, suspension and ease of manufacture. Sometimes these changes can be quite subtle as in the case of the German Panther, although its development was cut short by cessation of hostilities. On other occasions the vehicle changes appearance in a most dramatic fashion as in the American Sherman series of tanks.

When first put into large-scale production they were made by different manufacturers, who fitted various engines which made for different deck configurations and, in a couple of cases, different lengths of hull. Even when they shared the same engines, vehicles made by different manufacturers had totally different hulls, one being cast and one fabricated. As the type was developed the transmission cover was cast in one piece, the hull access hatches enlarged, the front hull revised upon fabricated versions, a cupola and loader's hatch added to the turret, a bigger gun fitted which required a new larger turret, and a new type of suspension fitted. The first types bore little resemblance to their final offspring. Add minor differences and various patterns of tracks and the situation becomes even more complex. Take into account extemporized armour, highly individual fittings and the British practice of fitting the potent seventeen-pounder anti-tank gun, and the situation becomes positively bewildering. And then there were all the variants. The simplest version was fitted with Duplex Drive flotation gear to allow the tank to 'swim' to shore. (Once on land, the flotation screen was blown away with explosives, and the tank could support the infantry at once.) Others were fitted with mine-exploding flails, or were converted into recovery vehicles, whilst others had close-support howitzers fitted instead of their normal main armament. The chassis was also used for a variety of purposes mainly as the mount for an artillery piece or as an armoured troop carrier.

Not only were the tanks developed but the basic chassis was usefully employed as the basis of a variety of other supporting types, such as recovery vehicles, self-propelled guns and assault engineer vehicles. This trend really took off in the Second World War and has continued ever since. During the last war some vehicles, especially German ones, were used exclusively as specialist types (i.e. anything but the basic gun tank or troop carrier) once their days of usefulness as tanks proper was at an end.

Today specialist vehicles such as engineer vehicles and self-propelled guns are based mainly upon the two most common types of chassis, those of the main battle tank and the armoured personnel carrier.

From the modeller's point of view this situation can be a tricky one. First of all, when a popular type is brought out in kit form it seems that no two modellers will ever agree that it was the right version. Take as an example the Tamiya kit Panzer III. It depicts one of the final production versions of the vehicle. At this stage in its cycle the vehicle was past its best and its days of glory, when it shattered the opposition, were gone. Instead it represented the last efforts to keep it competitive. In my opinion it would have been much better if an earlier model had been made which could have represented the vehicle in its heyday of the desert and early Russian campaigns. However the situation is redressed somewhat by the availability of the Stug III assault gun in model form. This variant, the most representative of all, depicts a latish version, in action from late '43 onwards, when the vehicle had changed its role from that of an infantry support weapon to that of a tank destroyer. In this guise the type made its main contribution to the German war effort.

Both the Sherman and the Panzer IV respectively the most widely manufactured types of America and Germany, are available in a decent variety of sub-variants. Italeri's splendid Sherman (actually a late M4 A1 76 mm) is in the form of a recovery, self-propelled 105 mm howitzer and an armoured troop carrier and is shortly to be available in another guise, whilst the equally impressive Tamiya model (in fact a mid/late M4 A3 75 mm, very typical of American vehicles in Europe) has sprouted another variant in the shape of the Jumbo assault tank. This makes seven different vehicles based upon the basic M4 chassis. Tamiya's Panzer IV is available in early and late varieties, indeed the early one is supplied with the wherewithal to be upgraded,

as was done in real life. It is also available as two types of SP anti-aircraft guns, two types of tank destroyer and as a heavy assault howitzer. The model manufacturers have, in effect, done the same as the tank makers; they have used their basic chassis as the basis of a variety of models. This is a very satisfying situation for the modeller who wishes to build up a variety of sub-types of a few basic vehicles. This is fine as far as it goes but, inevitably, as subject knowledge increases so does the urge to make more representative, specific or appealing vehicle models. But we are never, ever going to reach the stage where every variant of sub-type of every vehicle is available. If, for example, you want an early type of vehicle and only a late type is available as a kit then one must be converted. If a particular variant is not available the same applies – it is up to the modeller to make the model. Of course it calls for a greater degree of commitment, effort and the acquisition of new skills but it is a very satisfying part of the spectrum of modelmaking.

It might now be appropriate to deal in some depth with the subject of reference material.

References

The following sources of reference are relevant for conversions and scratch building work.

PUBLICATIONS

A search through the shelves of any large newsagent will unearth the hobby magazines. The best ones are, in Britain, *Military Modelling* and *Military Hobbies*, and in America, *Fine Scale Modelling*. It is a good idea to buy one of these magazines regularly, and within a year or so the beginnings of a reference library will emerge. Publications such as these contain reviews, background articles, illustrations and frequently relevant how-to-do-it features. Equally important to the newer modeller are the advertisements; all the specialist importers advertise as well as the larger manufacturers.

The next stage should be a trip to a specialist bookshop, even if it means quite a lengthy trip. There not only can one purchase individual titles but it is also possible to see some of the more specialist items available; much excellent material is published by German, Italian and Japanese concerns.

Unfortunately much of the AFV modeller's staple material is no longer in print. Bellona prints and Profile publications suffered a sad demise a long time ago. Bellona prints started off many modellers on the hobby; they were lovely drawings reproduced in 1/76th scale which matched Airfix products perfectly. Profile publications each gave fairly comprehensive coverage to a single tank and its derivatives and generally featured artwork of a high standard. The good news is that most of these illustrations have survived and are used to illustrate current books, frequently being revised in the light of new research. Currently the best specific references available are the Squadron/Signal 'Armour in Action' series. They deal comprehensively with one type of vehicle and give photographic scale and detail drawings and colour artwork coverage in addition to well-researched historical details. They cannot be bettered as basic source material and are the basis of most current reference collections. At present coverage is restricted to more important types.

Nor should general books be overlooked. These have generally been very well researched and illustrated with colour artwork. Valuable items include the Second World War photograph albums published by Patrick Stephens Ltd and the Areo publications 'Armour' series. They give extensive coverage in photographic

form and are just the thing for helping one interpret scale drawings. Weightier material can always be found. Try the local library and, if it is not on the shelves, it can be ordered.

CLUBS AND SOCIETIES

The best source of references are other modellers. It is possible to get in touch with other enthusiasts by joining the local group or its parent society. Try The Miniature Armoured Fighting Vehicles Association, whose address is given in the reference section (page 120). The AFV Society of North America is also a useful, if not so practical a group. The International Plastic Modellers' Society is not interested solely in AFV modelling. All these societies publish magazines, usually on a bi-monthly basis and many modellers join them specifically for this reason. The magazines contain fine scale drawings, reviews and a very good articles. However, the best reason of all for joining such an organization or society is to get in touch with like-minded folk. Most societies have local branches, and new members are made most welcome. Quite often the societies combine for the purposes of meetings, and when a newer modelmaker meets the 'veterans' it is always an eye-opener. The wealth of reference material that they have accumulated seems beyond belief. Normally they are only too delighted to allow access to this material and will gladly hunt out relevant sections so that notes or copies may be taken.

PRODUCING SCALE DRAWINGS

From the converter's point of view what is most needed are scale drawings from which to work. Whilst it is possible to get a fair number from the sources mentioned, the less popular types are not well represented in commercial outlets. However, there is a dedicated band of enthusi-

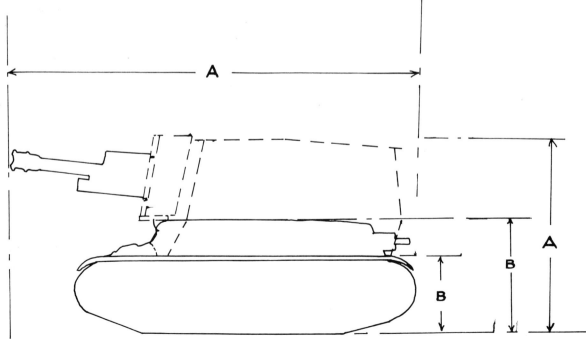

asts who produce scale drawings of the more esoteric types. Most of these drawings are adequate and some are quite exceptional. They are mostly advertised in the society/club magazines and usually cost next to nothing. A list of the most useful and easily available ones is to be found on page 119. If plans are not available then it is possible to draw your own or at least make working drawings. The minimum needed is a list of dimensions and some photographic coverage. This is made a great deal easier if one is converting an existing model into another variant because it is possible to relate the information to the basic model. When scratch building one must, literally, start from scratch.

Let us take as an example a real-life conversion such as those that the German army carried out on captured French Hotchkiss light tanks. Many of these were stripped of their turrets, then fitted with a 105 mm howitzer protected by an armoured superstructure. As far as I know the vehicle has never been fully documented but several good photographs of the type exist. The chassis is available in the form of the delightful Hellier model, so this can be made up and used as the basis of the plans. Find out the published dimensions of the vehicle, divide them by thirty-five and draw out a series of 'scale boxes', one of the vehicle's length by its height and the other two of its width by the height. (As the vehicle does not seem to have been photographed from overhead it would perhaps be a little optimistic to draw an overhead 'scale box'.

Draw in the chassis, and, working from *all* the available photographs, extend the drawing. Build it up by comparing the drawn and known

Facing page top: *This German conversion of a French Hotchkiss light tank to a self-propelled gun is poorly documented. I based this model on very limited information and got it nearly right. It is now in the process of being corrected as more information becomes available.*

Bottom: *A shows overall dimensions as given in a reference source; B the known model dimensions from a kit.*

information with the photographs. Angles may be measured using a protractor. Work away until a drawing that *looks right* starts to emerge; it is much more important to produce an effort which looks right than to expect to end up with a perfect scale drawing. If you are unhappy with the amount of information available wait until more comes to hand. The figure opposite shows how a drawing can make a model possible, even if information at first seems inadequate. In this instance it turned out that the model was basically correct and the extra details could be added once more information came to hand.

VEHICLES AS SOURCE MATERIAL

The final source of reference is, of course, the real thing. There may be physical difficulties encountered in travelling to a large collection, however, and there are other less obvious problems. Although it sounds weird, many museum exhibits are wrong: many foreign vehicles were captured or acquired in a damaged or incomplete state. They may have been 'bodged' to make them presentable as exhibits, or had damaged parts replaced from another vehicle in an even worse state of repair. The vehicle cannibalized might well have been an earlier or a later model and whilst the replacement parts fit, or can be made to fit, they may not be correct for that particular vehicle. Native vehicles might well have been used for experimental purposes such as testing a new engine, tracks or armament. Whilst it may well have been intended to convert the vehicle back to its original configuration the result will generally be subtly wrong and may very well be totally wrong. Some of the exhibits may have been rescued from the ranges where they were used as hard targets, with obvious detrimental effects. Other vehicles may have been used only for training and be missing a lot of the standard fittings that the fighting vehicles sported. The worst errors seem to occur when one vehicle is made up from the undamaged portions of two or more. This is much more common than one might suspect. I believe that a large proportion of museum vehicles are defective in some detail, although given the circumstances of their acquisition this is scarcely to be wondered at. Things are getting better, as many exhibits are being restored to their former glory in a most professional manner. Unfortunately it is a slow process.

To some extent it is easier to use drawings which were prepared for manufacturers' drawings, handbooks and captured examples when they were in new condition.

The level of reference material with which one feels happy is a matter of individual choice. Some modellers are content with a minimum of a few decent photographs and a list of dimensions, whilst others demand accurate scale drawings and complete photographic coverage.

Tools

Once you embark on conversions or scratch building you may be surprised to find that the main tools needed are those already owned: a knife, a steel rule, sandpaper, and/or Swiss files. The only real difference is that more use is made of them. There is, however, little doubt that a few extra items tend to make life simpler.

As more, and frequently heavier, cutting will be done a heavy duty knife such as a Stanley knife is very useful. It is an ideal tool for cutting the thicker gauges of plastic sheet and carrying out surgery upon kit parts which are generally quite thick.

Some form of modelling saw is an asset. Razor saws are perfect for cutting small parts, such as suspension arms, visors etc., away from main kit components. For more general work a small hacksaw is useful.

Another tool which may prove invaluable is a modelling drill. Many of these are sold in the form of a small tool kit with attachments to allow them to be used as saws, grinders, reamers, buffs and even lathes. In my opinion they are best regarded simply as drills and, whilst they are not used very often, when they are needed there really is no substitute for them.

A couple of small clamps and a modelling vice always come in useful – frequently substituting for a third hand!

A good-quality set-square, protractor and circle-maker are aids which all serious model-makers possess. A transparent ruler is much better than a steel one for measuring and drawing with. Another valuable item is a pair of sharp, springbow dividers; they are extremely good for cutting out discs from sheet. A scriber is another tool which is sometimes useful.

A final valuable aid is a calculator. Using this is the easiest way of scaling up, or down, plans; it also helps to establish scale from a drawing.

Many tools and aids can be improvised as described in the previous chapter. Most modellers hold parts together with adhesive tape if they are warped and likely to spring apart. Similarly, Bluetack holds parts in place whilst the adhesive dries out. Even objects such as the humble elastic band prove very useful at times. At the other end of the scale are the very exotic and specialized tools that the makers would like to assure us will revolutionize our working practices. Of course some of them are valuable tools but really only to the more advanced workers who first of all

The real thing. Note the generally poor standard of finish on this post-war Egyptian vehicle (Budge collection).

A beautifully restored Grant. Note the rough texture on the casement and turret (Budge collection).

Tracks do pick up a lot of muck (Budge collection).

have a need for them and secondly are skilled enough to be able to make proper use of them.

About the only item that I can recommend in this 'exotic' category is a set of rivet punches which enables scale rivets to be punched out of sheet very accurately and quickly. It is also quite good for making handwheel rims but, whilst the results given are very impressive indeed, it is perhaps an over-complex solution to a couple of simple problems. The same applies to a soldering iron or its rather more impressive relative the pyrogravure. In theory these have a multitude of uses such as adding battle damage, depicting weld seams and even constructional work in heavier gauge materials, but many modellers' experience of them is off-putting. By all means look at new products but only buy them if they offer a really useful solution to insuperable problems.

Materials

Materials required for both scratch building and conversion projects are the same and, again, very basic. They are sheet polystyrene, wood and filler. The last two were dealt with in the first chapter, but it may be appropriate to expand upon the modeller's mainstay, sheet polystyrene.

The thickest practical gauge of this material is 60 thou. It is most useful for building up basic structures where strength is essential or for cutting out parts, which again must be strong, such as suspension arms. 40 thou. is a very useful standard thickness. It is at its best when used for the main parts of vehicles such as hull sides, enclosed turrets, and the like. It is also by far the best thickness to be used when heat-forming parts. 30 and 20 thou. are good general-purpose building materials, especially when a crisp edge is essential. 20 thou. is particularly good at depicting a thinner

plate used for the open sides on armoured vehicles such as self-propelled guns and armoured personnel carriers where too great a thickness is very obvious. 10 thou. is fine for making small parts where scale thinness is obviously called for; it is also ideal for making small detail parts such as hinges and support stays. 5 thou. is the thinnest practical thickness available, and cannot be regarded as a general-purpose material. Having made that point, there is little doubt that a sheet held in stock comes in useful at times. It is good for making very small detail parts where an appearance of extreme fineness is wanted.

Other materials which will get their fair share of use are plastic rod and tube in a variety of thicknesses.

Conversion projects

TAMIYA T34/76 1943

As I remarked earlier, the Tamiya T34 is considered by many modellers to be Tamiya's finest-ever model. It is accurate, well researched and, best of all, seems designed to please the modelmaker. There are three versions available of the tank proper, that is, of vehicles with turrets. Of these the best overall is the 1943 production model. It is not that much more accurate than the other versions; what is special about it are the variations of the basic vehicle which are available even when built 'straight from the box'. There is a choice of turret roofs, the early and the late pattern. There is also a choice of the patterns of roadwheel, as on the real vehicle. Optional fuel tank types may be fitted. The trackguards are depicted in their usual, battered, state as are the cylindrical fuel containers. There are several optional stowage items, including two

splendid unditching logs, and a very pleasing crew. All told it is an excellent model. The turret shown is the hard-edged type, possibly the least handsome of those available. The soft-edged turret is a little more pleasing to the eye whilst the cast (Ch.T.Z – the common abbreviation for the factory where these turrets were manufactured) is the most striking of all.

A resin-cast version of this particular turret is available from Miniature Armour Conversions. It comes in two parts with quite good instructions. The parts in my example of this kit were not a very good fit as supplied; indeed, they needed a good deal of trimming before they would fit together and then a healthy application of filler to hide the gaps. Once the filler was sanded smooth however, the kit looked very accurate and handsome. The kit

The Top Brass cast turret fitted. Although handsome, it is not really accurate and needs quite a bit of filing and sanding before it can be considered acceptable. Note the air-inlet grills on the engine decking, which have been cut out and replaced with wire mesh.

turret parts can be glued directly to the resin parts using either tube cement, or better, contact adhesive.

This is a very simple conversion, one of a type that the supporting cottage industry is producing. It is an ideal first project for those modellers who want to 'test the water'. Although it is well worth having and it alters the model's appearance for the better. The option for those who consider the product too pricey is to modify the turret from the kit by assembling it, rubbing and carving it to shape

then building it up, as necessary, with a little filler.

THE STURMPANZER IV BRUMMBAER

This vehicle was based upon a requirement drawn up during the vicious street fighting which occurred in Stalingrad. It called for a heavily armoured vehicle armed with a howitzer of medium calibre which could be used to demolish strongpoints, fortified houses and the like. It was based on the Panzer IV and the standard 15 cm infantry howitzer was mounted within a heavily armoured box-like superstructure. It was quite effective in its intended role but the chassis was at its absolute weight limit. It is generally accepted that only between forty and sixty of these vehicles were built and as they were constantly being improved as they were produced, late versions were very different from early ones. Even though so few vehicles were made they are definitely of interest to military vehicle modellers.

Tamiya make a very good model of an early vehicle based upon their Panzer IV chassis. Many modellers decided that it would be nice to have a late version of the vehicle with a revised superstructure, the gun in a long-armoured collar, a ball mounted machine gun in the superstructure and all steel pattern road wheels. It was obvious that a conversion kit of this nature would be a success as far as the cottage industry was concerned and, sure enough, one is in production. It is made by ARBA Models but costs about two and a half

Facing page top: *The completed model showing a rough, and typical, winter finish hastily applied over the base dark green. Bottom: Arba Models' Brummbaer conversion is very complete as can be seen. It is also of very high quality. Model by David Parker.*

times the price of the basic model. On the other hand, the conversion is done extremely well and is very complete.

As the superstructure was shorter on the late-pattern vehicles, to compensate for the increased weight of the heavier armour used, the decision was taken to produce the superstructure and engine decking as one complete unit. The casting itself is very accurate and extremely well detailed. It is also very strong, being a pretty massive casting. It fits the kit chassis perfectly once the few casting plugs are cut off and thus the conversion is simplicity itself to carry out. The gun fits in any required position and it would not take much effort to make it movable. A pack of all-steel pattern road wheels is included.

The work involves fitting the gun into the superstructure and then attaching the part to the kit chassis with a drop of superglue, although contact adhesive is just as good and a little less final. The steel road wheels are super-glued to the kit suspension arms and the basic conversion is all ready to paint. Most vehicles seem to have worn a comprehensive coating of Zimmerit, which can be applied as described on page 37. If skirting armour is to be fitted, and most vehicles seem to have carried it, then it is a nice idea to make it and its supports out of thin-gauge sheet. 10 thou. is ideal, and gives a 'scalish' appearance.

THE LATE PATTERN M4 SHERMAN

One of the most famous tanks ever built, the Sherman was so thoroughly developed that late vehicles bore only a superficial resemblance to the earliest vehicles first blooded by British forces during the desert campaign. The M4 series was built by a large number of firms. The M4 itself was a standard type in production throughout the American involve-

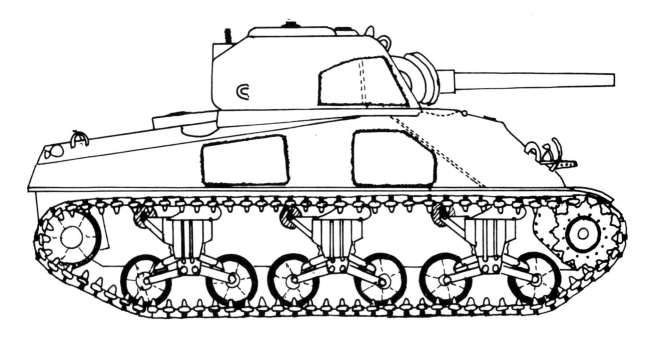

Sherman plans. Late model M4 with cast hull front.

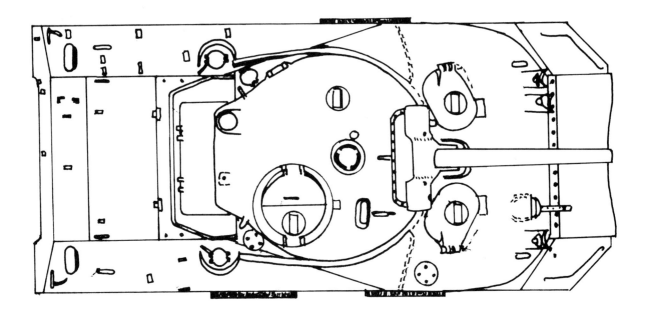

The late-pattern M4: note the texture on the carved turret.

ment in the war. In fact it was the first production model, because at first it was easier to fabricate the hull from plate than to produce the huge cast hull upper that with which the type had been designed. The cast hulled version was the next type to be put into production and was designated the M4 A1. It was also a standard type with a long production history. It was identical to the M4 except for the cast hull. Later versions of the M4 had a cast upper hull front section. This particular version of the M4 was not in production for very long but a large number were made and it was a most familiar vehicle. This vehicle is the subject of this conversion. It is based upon the excellent Italeri late M4 A1 and, as can be seen, it completely alters the model's appearance.

The Sherman (the general name given by the British to the M4 family) has been the subject of more cottage-industry activity than any other vehicle. Different patterns of turrets, hulls, alternative suspension units, tracks and etched brass 'super detailing' sets abound. They come in a variety of prices, none of them cheap, and are executed in a similar variety of degrees of competence. Oddly enough, some of the rather better presented and made ones are the least accurate. This conversion ignores all this 'assistance'. In many ways it is a traditional conversion in which the modeller starts off with a kit, some raw materials and tools and carries out the process himself.

Working method
Before lifting the modelling knife it is a good idea to study the scale and the working drawings to get some idea of what is involved.

Begin by assembling the kit chassis; the only point which needs watching is to make sure that the mould marks, which are very prominent, are removed by sanding from the road wheel tyres.

THE HULL
The hull should be tackled next. The figure beneath shows the areas of the hull which must be removed. Saw into the hull at the two points shown up to the turret splash guard. Gently cut between the cuts, following the line of the

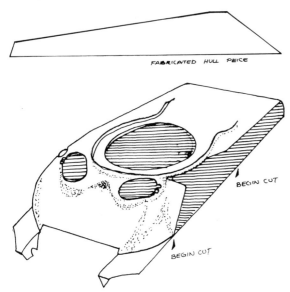

FABRICATED HULL PEICE

BEGIN CUT

BEGIN CUT

Remove shaded areas as shown, using scale drawings as reference.

splashguard, and remove this area. It is quite easy to cut through even this thick plastic. Make a light cut at first. As too much pressure is not being applied it is easy to follow the curve, and this initial cut will act as a guide for the next, heavier cuts. Never try to hack through the plastic all in one go; it is all too simple to make a mess of things and deform the hull. Clean up all four edges.

Now, remove the remaining hull sides to the rear of the cuts by, again, gently cutting through the plastic. The steel rule can be secured in position relative to the hull with a couple of blobs of Bluetack; otherwise it tends to slide all over the place, making for less than accurate cutting.

Finally, remove the rear plate. Referring to the scale drawings, or easier still the templates provided, cut out two hull sides, two upper hull parts and a backplate. It is best to trace them out and transfer the tracing onto the sheet, in this case 30 thou. Cut them out using a rule as a cutting guide except, of course, where the parts are curved. Spread your fingers well over the rule to ensure an even pressure all over and make the initial cuts, as always, light ones. You will notice that cutting through a substantial thickness of sheet raises 'burrs' or 'rags' at the cut edges. These should always be carefully rubbed away. When making two identical parts *always* check them against the scale drawing and equally importantly, *against each other*. A simple precaution like this can save a lot of heartache later on.

Cement the parts to the hull in the following order: top pieces, rear plate, then hull sides. The parts are best held in position with Bluetack (Presstick in the US) whilst they are drying out. This ensures that the hull will dry out true and square. Note the prominent weld where the cast part of the hull joins the fabricated area. This is easily depicted by 'nicking' the join with an old knife blade heated

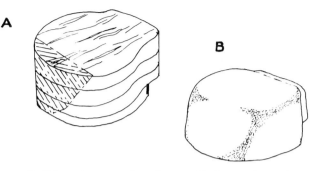

Build up the turret from layers of balsa as shown in A. Carve and sand to shape (B).

so that it melts the plastic fairly easily. Fill any gaps or 'fall offs' where the cast kit hull portions do not quite match up to your fabricated parts. Fit the new upper hull to the chassis and, when thoroughly dried out, gently sand the filler smooth. Fit all the detailing parts to the hull and put this now completed part to one side.

THE TURRET

Now for the turret. By far the easiest method is to use that of the Tamiya M4 A3. It is just about right and only needs the loader's hatch filling in and the angle of the turret bustle steepening to make it perfect. It is also a particularly pleasing turret. It is also possible to buy one cast in resin, but this costs about half as much again as the kit. A much more attractive method is to make one up from balsa wood, a material, at present, somewhat neglected by the mainstream of modelmakers. It is best to build the turret by laminating it from sheet. As the figure on the left shows, three 'plan' views in 6 mm (¼ in.) laminations

The model (left) compared to its 'parent'.

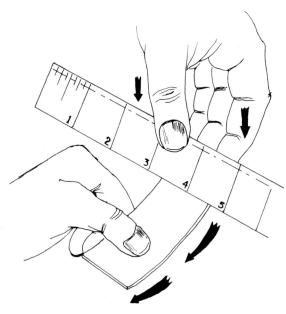

Pull thin plastic-sheet strips under a ruler to induce a curve. Press down firmly on the ruler whilst pulling through the plastic sheet.

smooth, hard surface. If all the grain is not totally invisible, repeat the process. The various bits from the kit can now be added where relevant. The main two are the commander's hatch and the spent-case ejection port but quite a number of other parts may also be utilized. The plate on the front of the turret is best cut from 10 thou. sheet and bonded to the filled wooden surface with contact adhesive, as are all plastic parts. The bulged recuperator housing which fits onto this plate should now be made up. Simply carve and finish it from a scrap of balsa as for the turret.

The final remaining problem is the gun mantlet. Cut a long strip of 30 thou. card at least 40 mm (1½ in.) wide. Lay it on the modelling board, take hold of one end with one hand and press down on it firmly with a wooden or plastic ruler in the other. Pull the strip under the ruler whilst still pressing

make up the main body of the turret, with an ⅛-inch thick circular one as the base. Bond them together with white glue, then allow to dry out for at least twenty-four hours. Balsa is an easy wood to work with but beware: don't be over-enthusiastic when sanding it.

Once the unit has dried out, saw away the front part to give a flat angled face then sand, using quite a coarse paper, to shape as shown in the figure on page 89. Finish off with a fine grade of paper until it is smooth.

FINISHING

The wood grain now needs filling. The best filler in a situation where the grain is not too extreme is a mix of talcum powder and thick enamel. Add sufficient talcum powder to the paint so that almost a paste results and spread it on with an old brush. Then it is very easy to sand it smooth with fine paper, which gives a

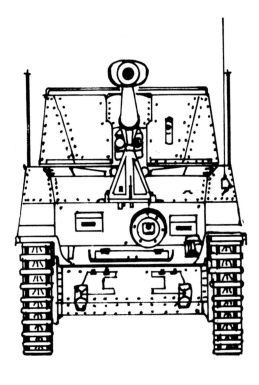

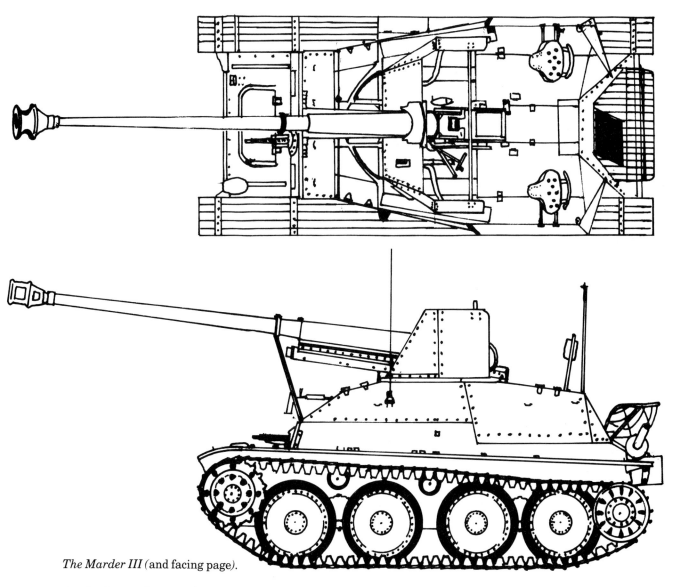

*The Marder III (*and facing page*).*

firmly down. Repeat the process several times and notice how the strip has assumed a distinct curve. The harder you push on the rule whilst pulling the strip through, the tighter the curve will be. When the correct curvature is obtained, make up the mantlet as shown; the central, raised part, will need its edges rubbed down to

a rounded form again as shown. The gun tube is cut down from the kit item.

Final touches such as appliqué armour and stowage are added, 30 thou. card giving a correct scale appearance of thickness for the first of these items.

The finished model is impressive and

The Marder III in the desert. Note the hastily applied sand finish typical of this theatre of operations.

original. Most important of all, however, it is a pleasant model to make up.

THE MARDER III (Sd Kfz 139)

When Germany invaded Russia the quality of the latest Russian tanks came as a very rude surprise. The mighty T34 and the KVI completely outclassed all current German tanks and indeed made them obsolete over-night. It became obvious that light vehicles such as the Panzer II and the 38(t) could no longer live on the battlefield and, as the pressing need was for heavy, mobile anti-tank weapons, these vehicles were used as the basis for them. The only weapons which could deal effectively with the new generation of Russian vehicles were the famous '88' anti-aircraft gun and the Russian 76.2 mm divisional gun, captured in large numbers. The latter weapons were slightly modified and hastily fitted to surplus Panzer II and 38(t) chassis. The 38(t) tank was very suitable as a conversion subject as the turret and bolted roof could very easily be removed and the complete Russian gun, minus its wheels, installed. A new armour superstructure was fitted and the gunshield modified to give extra, if fragile, protection to

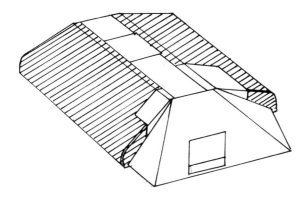

Areas to be removed from the kit engine deck.

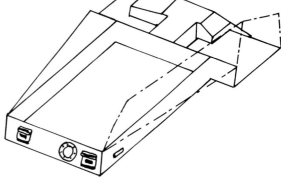

General view of the superstructure showing new parts.

the crew. Although very much a makeshift solution it was, in the hands of skilled crew, quite an effective weapon.

The resulting vehicle was certainly an unusual-looking item and one which modellers find fascinating. This conversion is based upon the Italeri late-pattern Marder III with 7.5 cm PAK 40 kit and is typical of this type of conversion which indeed largely reflects the full-sized practice. The basic model was not one of Italeri's better efforts. There is a very clumsy joint on the driver's plate which needs filling and the road wheels are rather oversized. The model has inherited this last feature from the lead model in the series the Panzer Jager 'Hetzer' which was, conversely, the last highly developed version of this chassis. To allow for the extra weight the running gear was enlarged by about 10 per cent and this was faithfully reproduced in miniature. The same running gear was used for the other two model variants and whilst it is not really correct it looks very right.

Working method
Begin, as usual, by carefully studying the drawings, especially the general rear view. Assemble the basic chassis and hull, deleting

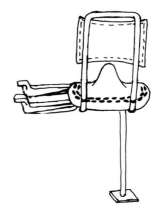

The seat.

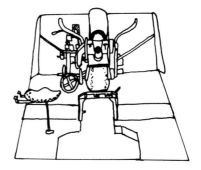

General view of the rear of the vehicle fighting compartment.

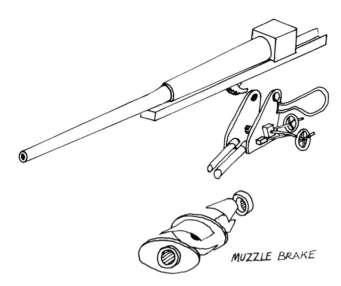

Breakdown of a gun into its basic parts: tube, breech block, cradle recuperator, housing muzzle etc.

MUZZLE BRAKE

the hull roof and engine decking. Fill in the gap in the driver's plate with a scrap of 40 thou. and sand it smooth. Install a flat plate made from 20 thou. sheet; you can measure the exact dimensions from the *plan* view, and this plate effectively forms the floor of the fighting compartment. The next step is to fit the triangular bottom plates, for the new forward superstructure, to the top of the crew compartment. These triangular pieces are, relatively, very long and shallow and extend from the front plate to the far edge of the fighting compartment. Again it is best to make them out of 20 thou. Finally, fill the 'steps' between the two new pieces on each side with a scrap of the same material.

GUN MOUNTING

A gun mounting is now needed. Italeri make three versions of the same vehicle with the tank proper and the later pattern Marder III

being the best for conversion purposes. The Marder III is more suitable as a conversion subject as it contains the necessary gun mounting cruciform, and the gun provided yields up several useful parts. The rear basket is also featured in this kit. I based my model upon the tank kit as the turret was wanted for another project. Install the cruciform and then turn your attention to the rear decking. Cut away the kit engine decking as shown, install the small piece left, propping it up in position with a piece of Bluetack, then sheet it in with 10 thou.

THE SUPERSTRUCTURE

The superstructure may now be tackled. Working from the plans, cut out the side pieces and the front plate from 20 thou.; check identical parts against each other, as always, to make sure that they are exactly the same. Fit these pieces carefully using a very small amount of liquid cement. Make sure that this structure is even and balanced. The split hatches may be modelled open or closed. Note that the driving area is not fully enclosed, the driver and co-driver being protected only by the hatches themselves overhead. At this stage an attempt should be made to add some form of interior detail. The main parts visible are the long ammunition stowage boxes at the sides of the superstructure. These are easily fabricated from 20 thou. and installed, as is a splash bar just behind the driving compartment. Cut from 20 thou. two triangular plates and fit them on to the rear of the new superstructure. The basic superstructure is now complete.

THE GUN

The gun should now be tackled. It looks quite complicated and, in truth, it is. It is not strictly necessary, however, to reproduce an exact miniature of the object; what is needed is a gun that looks right and is dimensionally correct.

Then again any complicated structure is made up of a number of simple sub-units. If we split the gun down to these sub-units we find the tube, the recuperator, the breech, the trunnion mount, the muzzle brake and the elevating and sighting gear. The tube is made in two parts. It is best to use plastic tubing. Carefully cut the length of the rear segment, making sure that the cut is true and clean. The front part of the tube is tapered and this may be achieved by scraping with a heavy craft knife as illustrated on p. 105. It is not at all difficult and when it is about right the tube can simply be smoothed off with a medium-fine grade of sandpaper. The smoothness can be maintained by wrapping the paper tightly about the tube and twisting the tube against it. Cement the two parts of the tube together; it helps align them correctly if they are joined together with a central length of rod. The breech in the kit looks reasonably correct except that it is a bit more massive than

it should be; however, it is easily trimmed to shape.

The recuperator cover is simply made from 20 thou. and fitted. It is best to decorate it with strips of 10 thou. and slices of rod or tube. The gun cradle should now be made. Note that, in essence, it consists of two side pieces and a base plate; make these parts from 30 thou. When making up these 'open' parts it is essential to use the minimal amount of cement and to allow them to dry out completely, otherwise they can very easily distort. That is the last thing any modeller wants. The muzzle brake could be modified from the kit part very easily, or one can be made from scratch as shown. Details such as handwheels, sights and so on can be had from the kit whilst parts such as guards and the elevating arc are easily cut from sheet. Make up the gunshield from 20 thou. and when firmly set, attach it in position on the gun with a couple of blobs of Bluetack.

Basic construction of the vehicle showing the cruciform mounting the gun and the new superstructure being fitted. Note the gun and shield and all those lovely rivets!

Now attach the shield to the gun carriage with stays made of plastic rod. You find out how long the rod stays need to be by the old, old method of trial and error. Hold them in place with tweezers, secure them with a wash of cement and, once you are sure of them, set them aside for a couple of days to dry out. An extra wash of cement will ensure that the shield is firmly attached to the gun. Once the assembly is as strong as possible, carefully remove the Bluetack and fit the gun to the cruciform.

Another view of the vehicle shown 'supporting' four Italian troops.

RIVETING

Now the fun really starts! The vehicle's riveted construction was a very distinctive feature and it really must be depicted. There are four good ways of producing rivets:

1 It is now possible to buy a tool which punches rivets out of sheet. The resulting items are slightly domed and very realistic. This solution, though excellent, seems a little extreme.
2 If a piece of rod is held next to a heat source such as a lighted cigarette end or a hot soldering iron then the end of the rod will mushroom and give a very nice rivet. Chop

it off and complete with a piece of 'stalk'; drill a hole in the model the same diameter as the stalk, then insert the rivet and secure it with a wash of cement. This is an ideal method. Very demanding model-makers perfect this technique by inserting the rod into a 'click-stopped' propelling pencil. Each 'click' exposes about 0.75 mm of rod; three 'clicks' exposes enough rod for a decent-sized rivet head and a further two are enough for the stalk once the head has been formed. The cottage industry is now making these items pre-formed. It is quite an easy matter to mark out and drill a line or area of holes. Insert a good number of rivets, then secure them all in one go with a wash of cement.

3   Cut thin slices of rod, pick them up with the point of the knife, place a dab of cement on the model and then put the rivet in place. This method works well when one wants the riveted effect to stand out and is recommended for modellers attempting the exercise for the first time.

4   Plate the model with 5 thou. card/sheet upon which the rivet detail has been embossed with something like a school compass. The method, disliked by some, does work, gives a subtle effect and is perhaps suitable for smaller scale models.

There are of course dozens of other methods. Grains of salt or sugar, dabs of liquid plastic, or thick paint can be used and some modellers even go so far as to cut rivets off surplus or scrapped models. Another school of modellers circumnavigate the problem by taking the view that riveted detail would not show up in this scale – in many ways an entirely sensible attitude. Unfortunately, however, riveted detail *does* show up so it is largely up to the individual how the rivets are modelled.

FINAL DETAILS

Once the model is riveted it is just a case of adding final details and by now these will be self-explanatory. The gun-travelling crutch is easily knocked up from thin sheet and rod and the fighting-compartment weather-cover stays are simply made from lengths of rod. The only parts liable to give problems are the seats for the crew in the fighting compartment. They were of the type used in agricultural machinery and are conspicuous. If you fit a crew and show them seated as if enjoying the view, then they are hidden so it doesn't really matter if they are accurately modelled or not; but it seems that the backrests were usually removed, stowed in the basket and the seats slung over the sides where they do show prominently. Fortunately, there is a fairly easy way out which also provides a painless introduction into the art of heat-forming plastic sheet. Treat yourself to a cigar, one of those that comes in a large, torpedo-shaped, aluminium case. Stand the cigar tube on its end making sure that it is firmly fixed to the baseboard with a few blobs of Bluetack then take a good-sized piece of 30 thou. sheet. Hold the piece of sheet over a match and rotate its middle area, making sure that it does not come into contact with the flame. When the plastic becomes floppy, it usually begins to smoke and blacken; put out the match, grasp the sheet in both hands then pull it gently over the rounded end of the tube. Allow it to cool for a few seconds and you will have a concave indentation in the sheet. Repeat the process, scribe the parts out, drill them and mount them in place. It's as easy as that.

In all, this is quite a difficult conversion. In effect, the model from the chassis and hull up has been scratch built. Once you can tackle a model of this nature, then you are ready to proceed to the ultimate stage of the hobby, scratch building.

4 Scratch Building

In the eyes of most experienced modelmakers there is little doubt that building a model from scratch is the highest form of modelmaking. It is also, by far, the most personally satisfying.

To a large extent it is a natural progression from assembling kits and converting them as discussed in the previous chapters. By the time you get round to scratch building the way a vehicle is put together is quite obvious, so in that respect at least you are not really starting from scratch!

In the past one had to scratch build if one wanted a representative collection of models. The situation has now dramatically improved with a wide choice of quality models available and the need for scratch building has greatly diminished. However, as the individual's knowledge grows certain subjects, which will never be commercial propositions as models, begin to appeal. The art of scratch building is easily acquired. It is also by far the most enjoyable form of modelmaking that there is.

Tools and materials are exactly the same as those discussed in the previous section and references are much the same. You really never can have too many sources of information.

Before embarking on a scratch-built model, gather together all the reference material that you can and study it. If possible, compare it to a model kit of similar type and see how the manufacturers have tackled the subject; is there anything that can be learnt from it? Materials will be obvious, but check to see if parts which would be difficult to fabricate can be culled from a kit. Frequently the running gear of a kit can be used with a little modification, as can items such as tracks, cupolas, armament and tools and fittings. This may mean scrapping a kit for its running gear which sounds wasteful but, in effect, the finished model has cost the price of a kit plus a few coppers for plastic, card, wood, filler etc. From the rest of the kit useful pieces such as machine guns, vision slots, wheels, grab handles and the like can be salvaged and may come in handy later on.

Scratch building projects

THE US M59 ARMOURED PERSONNEL CARRIER

This model is of the vehicle which was the ancestor of the current type of tracked 'battle taxi'. They have given excellent service and are probably the most widely used type of armoured vehicle in the Western alliance. Although the type is being replaced by the mechanized infantry fighting vehicle, a much more heavily armed and expensive vehicle, the M113 (the M59's direct descendant) will be in service for a long time into the future.

Although the M59 did not have a long service life by current standards it was the trendsetter and was manufactured in large numbers. As a model it is a simple 'boxy' subject, albeit a handsome one. It is an ideal first project and acts as a basis for more advanced models as all the basic techniques are involved in its construction.

General view of the M59 construction. Note the reinforcing bulkheads in the lower chassis pan.

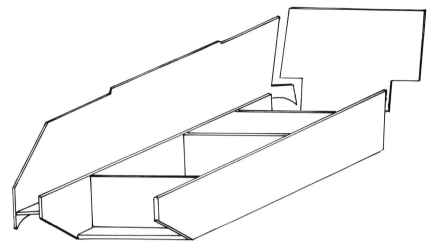

The basis of any scratch-built model is the chassis pan. It must be made as strong and true as possible. Any errors such as slight dimensional ones, warping or a lack of squareness might not be readily apparent yet, if unnoticed, they will 'magnify' and spoil the model as it grows. The point has been made several times before, but it is worth repeating: when two or more identical parts are required, check them against each other to *make sure* that they are *exactly* the same. If a piece has to have square corners check them with a set-square. Always work from a flat baseboard; if a part such as the chassis floor must be flat

check it against the flat modelling baseboard to ensure that it is. When fitting parts at 90 degrees to each other, such as the sides to the floor secure the floor plate to the modelling baseboard with a length of Twinstick (double-sided adhesive tape) or similar material then fit the sides, ensure that they are square on with a set-square and hold them in position with small blobs of Bluetack until the unit has thoroughly dried out. Where plates meet each other at an angle make sure that the edges are chamfered, as shown below, to ensure a snug and strong join. Where parts need to have detail scribed into them, such as on the nose

Mitre edges by drawing plastic sheet gently over sandpaper (A). This gives joins which are strong (see B) and unlikely to collapse, as in C.

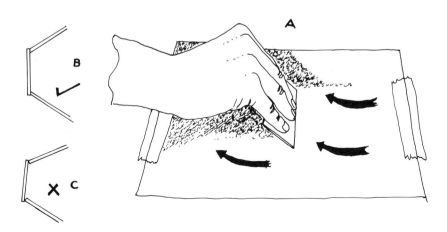

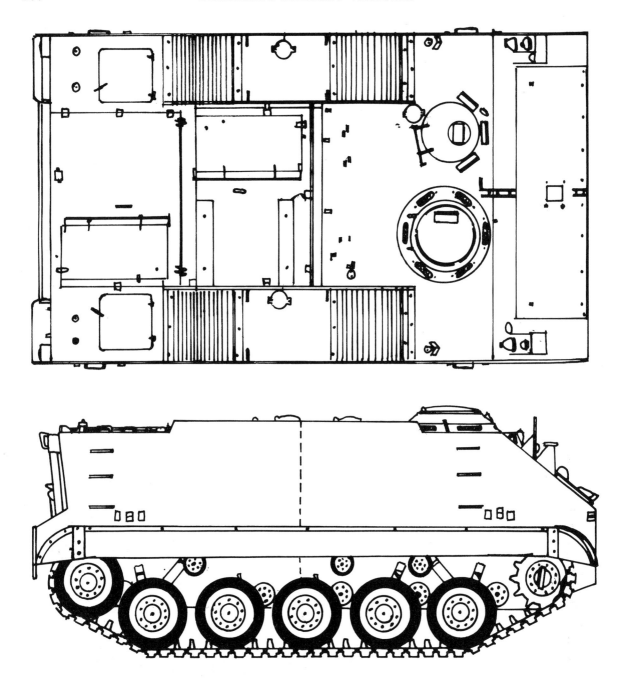

Facing: *The M59 is a simple, boxy but attractive model. Extensive weathering helps it to stand out.*

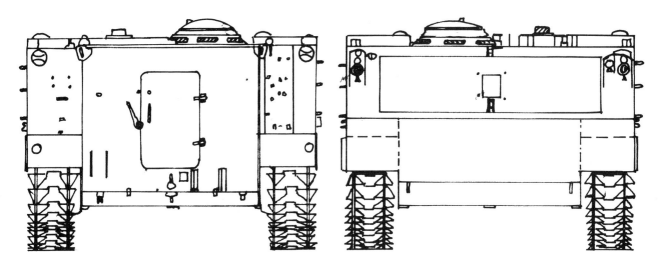

(The above drawings are not to scale and should be used only as a guide.)

The M59 from the upper rear. Note the configuration of the rear trackguards.

plate on this model, scribe them when the plate is cut out and not when it is part of the constructed model. Make all these points standard working practices.

Working method
Begin this model by laying down the chassis floor from 60 thou. The chassis walls will be made from 40 thou., so allow for their thickness when marking out the parts. Cut the sides from 40 thou. and cement them in position. Make up some bulkheads as shown, also from 40 thou., and fit them as in page 99 (top). These parts greatly add to the model's strength and help ensure that vital squareness. Next cut out and fit the chin plate from 40 thou., remembering to mitre the edges where it meets the floor and will meet the nose plate. Now cut out the nose and rear plates from 40 thou., allowing for the thickness of the chassis sides and floor when cutting out the rear part. Scribe the relevant detail on the nose plate and then cement both parts in position.

If this is a first-time scratch build, it is best

to build the model closed down. This is first of all simpler to do and secondly it allows the construction of the model to be sturdy. Bearing these factors in mind, install a sheet of 30 thou. across the full length and width of the chassis, only allowing for the thickness of the hull sides which will be made from 30 thou. Lengthwise it should fit snugly up to the nose and rear plates. Following the example of the chassis, it is advisable to install a couple of full-height bulkheads made from 40 thou. Cut and fit the side plates then the roof, which should have the relevant detail scribed in, from the same material. Finally, fit the glacis plate from 40 thou., and the basic 'box' is built. If it has been carefully constructed this structure will be immensely strong, at the very least as strong as a similar kit.

It is quite an easy task to detail up the model. Whilst it is possible to engrave hatch and door detail, it is equally viable to depict it using 10 thou. sheet. Obviously this stands slightly proud but then so do most hatches and they are effective when depicted in this manner.

The air-intake louvres are made up from Microstrip (pre-sliced strip sheet polystyrene). Each length is best positioned with pointed tweezers and secured with a wash of cement.

If you are pleased with the standard of the model you won't mind buying the kit which must be cannibalized to provide the running gear. There are two alternatives; the model shown utilized the Tamiya M41, a quite elderly but still very respectable kit. However, it would be far better to use the much newer, and cheaper, Italeri 'Chaffee' model as this kit also

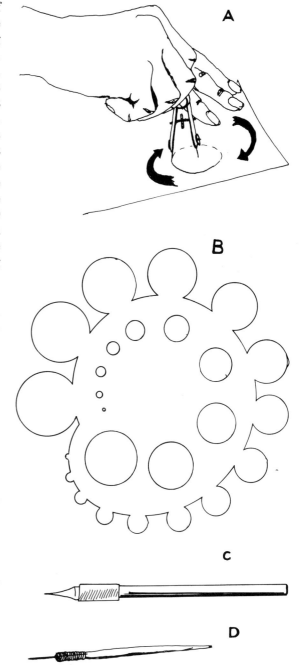

Scribe a circle (A) by using sharp springbow dividers; or (B) use a circle-maker and a bought scriber (C); or make up your own scriber (D) by lashing a darning needle to an old paintbrush shaft.

includes the correct pattern of cupola. In either case remove the suspension arms, (it was necessary to saw them off the M41) and fit them to the chassis, prop up the scratch-built hull on a piece of wood so that the model is not resting on the suspension arms, and allow it to dry out. An extra dab of cement can't harm and will help ensure that these parts are firmly fixed.

Quite a few parts from the kit can be used to help detail the model. Items such as the headlamps, grab handles and the rear lights are exactly the right pattern, so use them.

Once the model *seems* to be completed, check it over to make sure that all the necessary detail is included. When it is painted and the tracks are fitted the model is complete. It is a very handsome, if simple, model and owes its existence to the builder's efforts, not those of a kit manufacturer.

THE 'BISON' 15 CM SELF-PROPELLED GUN

Although the Panzer 38(t) was obsolete as a tank by 1941 the type had greatly impressed the German armoured troops with its general durability, its extreme reliability and its ease of manufacture. As they had the manufacturing facilities available, the type was redesigned by moving the engine forward, thus leaving the rear of the vehicle free for mounting weapons. The original intention was to mount the heavy Sig.33 heavy infantry howitzer but in the event the majority of the type mounted the PAK 40 anti-tank gun. Even so, no fewer than 370 of the howitzer-armed versions were completed and they were a most important and useful vehicle.

The basis of the model is the familiar Italeri 38(t). Whilst it would be possible to convert the chassis, it is far easier and better to scratch build the vehicle using only the running gear, trackguards and detail parts from this splendidly useful kit.

Working method
Begin by making a very strong chassis pan as described in the previous project. Note, however, that the vehicle is open-topped and it is not possible to reinforce it with internal bulkheads; so you need to build it as strong as you possibly can and constantly check that the structure is crisp and square. Once the basic hull is completed, build up the superstructure from 20 thou. which gives a nice 'scale thickness' effect and yet is sufficiently sturdy for its designated task. This gauge of material is a particularly useful one and is strong enough to allow medium-sized free-standing structures to be built. Its main limitation is that large, unsupported areas tend to bow, which puts a realistic appearance somewhat at risk! The parts shown here are about as large as should be used without being supported.

Two types of driver's compartment top are used: a fabricated one and, later, a cast one. The cast one, as used on this model, is simplicity itself to make. Cut out a front portion, a top plate and two side pieces from 40 thou. Cement them together and trial fit the unit to the glacis plate to make sure that it fits

Build up the basic structure, as shown.

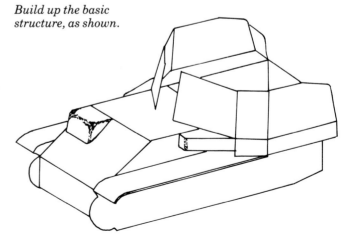

Taper a thick plastic tube to give a gun barrel, by scraping away from you with a craft knife.

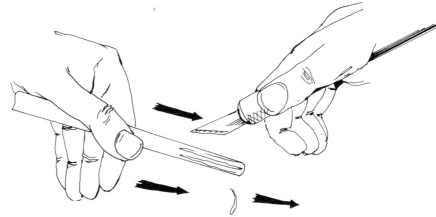

as it should. Give the joins an extra brushing over with cement in order to weld them together firmly then put the piece to one side for at least forty-eight hours. Once it is completely dry, sand the edges until the cast effect is achieved.

Cut down the mudguards from the kit and cement them firmly in place; then add all the detail and kit parts where applicable. Again, parts such as the gun travelling crutch and lifting handles are easily made up from scraps of sheet and rod. It is best to add the rivet detail at this point.

The gun is not such a difficult project as it first seems. Study the working drawing. Note that the gun is essentially a sturdy and simple piece of equipment. The barrel is shaped from a length of tube. Pick a piece of tubing with fairly thick walls and scrape away – a Stanley-type knife is best for this operation. Try to ensure that the amount of plastic scraped away is even around the thickness of the walls. The collar is easily made from a block of plastic. To make the block, laminate three thicknesses of 40

A

B

C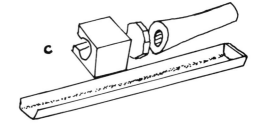

D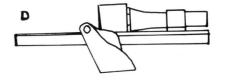

Begin to build up the gun as in A by cementing a disc of card to a length of tubing. Fill in to shape with Milliput or Greenstuff, then sand smooth as in B. Add other parts as in C and D.

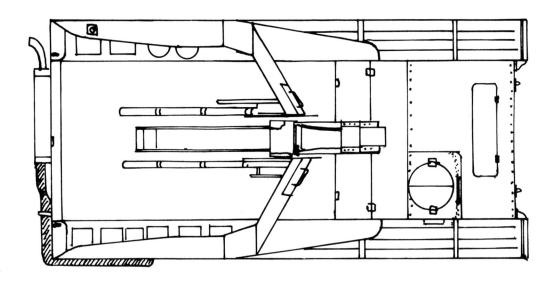

Bison plans.

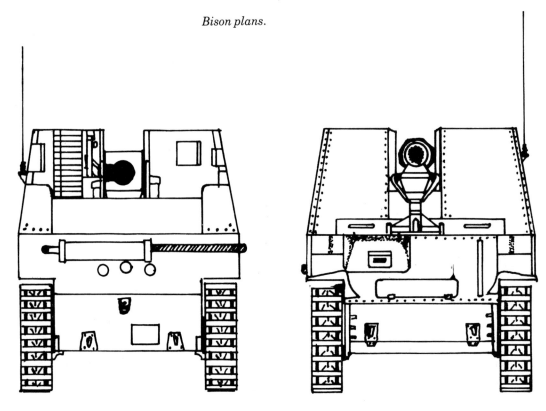

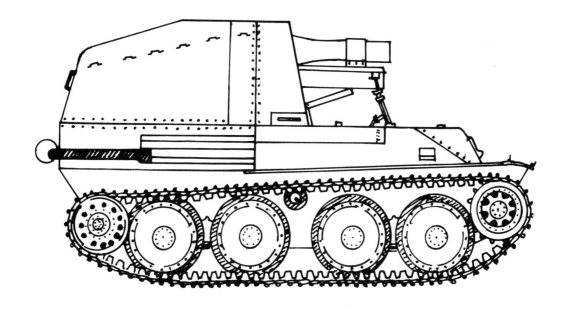

Below: *The Bison 'skulking' and looking very dirty and war-weary.*

thou., allow to dry out thoroughly, then carve to shape. The massive breech block is constructed in a similar manner. Make up the recuperator from 40 thou. and the trunnion cradle from the same material. It is best to make the recoil tubes from lengths of sprue with 'collars' of tubing pushed on. Handwheels are easily made up from punched discs of 20 thou. and scraps of rod. The ammunition boxes are easily knocked up out of 20 thou., a tedious but necessary process.

It is possible to use the kit exhaust box but a long pipe must be formed. Use a length of sprue and heat it where it needs to be formed using a match or gas lighter set on its lowest setting. When the sprue just begins to droop, bend it to shape: the sprue needs bending in two places.

All that now remains is to cut the running gear from the kit chassis, thin the mounts down to thickness and fit them and the running gear in position.

This is one model which greatly benefits from a crew – otherwise it tends to look bare. At first it seems rather a daunting project but it is easily made using basic scratch building methods learned upon simple projects such as the previous one. Whilst it may not be an ideal first subject, it certainly is a fine second one!

Note how the crew bring the model to life.

THE RUSSIAN T26B

The T26B was derived from a Vickers commercial design, the famous six-tonner. The Vickers design enjoyed a good deal of commercial success in the '30s and was bought and developed by several nations. Probably the most famous series was the Russian one, which developed the vehicle from the original twin-turreted design to a much more powerfully armed vehicle with a larger single turret. The vehicle was manufactured in huge numbers and gained a fearsome reputation when it was involved in the Spanish civil war. It was much more powerful than the light tanks supplied by the Axis powers to the Nationalist side and could deal with them with ease.

By the start of the German invasion of Russia the T26B was no longer in the first league; it had thin armour and its firepower was not as good as the latest German designs. However, it had been superseded in production by vastly improved types: the Russian army had absorbed the lessons of their vehicle combat experience very well indeed and had acted upon them.

Whilst it is a very worthy subject for a model the T26B is rather a difficult one to build. It requires a good deal of time and effort but it is an immensely satisfying model to build. If a modeller can make a decent job of a model of this degree of constructional difficulty then no other projects will hold any fear.

A model of a subject as important as this would, one would think, have attracted the manufacturers. Unfortunately, however, it lacks the 'glamour' of the bigger, later and more successful types. There is a resin version made but it is difficult to obtain. Besides all this, scratch building offers the chance to show the vehicle 'opened up'.

The hull presents few problems, the turret only a few, easily resolved ones but the gun mantlet and the running gear do require some fairly complex solutions to the problems that they set.

Working method

THE HULL

Begin by cutting out the hull floor from 40 thou., allowing, as usual, for the thickness of the sides and the rear plate. The chin plate will be mitred to fit so there is no need to allow for this. As the model is to be built opened up there is no possibility of adding the usual mass of bulkheads to strengthen the structure, so make sure that the side pieces are really flat. One very useful bulkhead can, however, be introduced where the fighting compartment ends and the engine compartment begins; simply extend the rear plate down to the hull floor. Fit the rear deck with the relevant detail engraved upon it then fit the chin, nose and glacis plates, all from 30 thou. sheet. (In fact 20 thou. would be a more appropriate thickness for scale appearance, but 30 thou. is rather safer.) Cut and fit the front plate of the fighting compartment from the same material, then turn your attention to the roof.

Cut this piece from 30 thou. and cut out the turret ring aperture. It is best to scribe this out gently using springbow dividers rather than a circle-maker (see figure p. 103). Sometimes, when a large area is removed from within a piece, the part distorts, especially if the cutting out is done in a heavy-handed manner. Check that the part is flat, and if it is not then immerse it in hot water for a few seconds and press it flat under a pile of books. When it has cooled down the part will be perfectly flat. Carefully fit the roof, if necessary supporting it at the corners with small blocks of sheet to ensure that it is perfectly positioned in relation to the sides. Put the unit to one side and allow to dry out; you should now have a crisp and true structure.

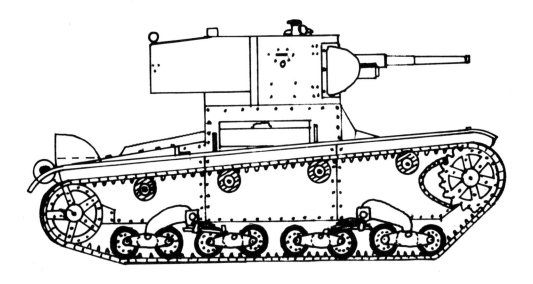

The T26.

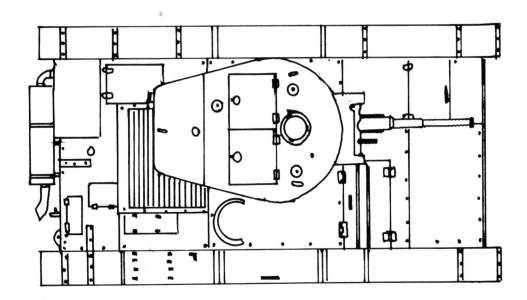

Facing page: *Note the fine lines of the T26, the sharp
construction and delicate suspension.*

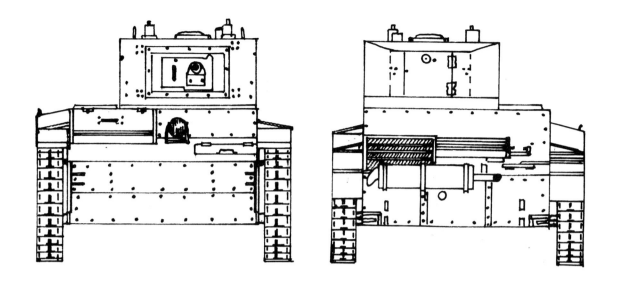

THE TURRET

It is best to tackle the turret next. Begin by cutting two top views out of 30 thou. Cut the hatches out of one and the turret ring out of the other as previously described. As can be seen from the plan (figure p. 110) the base of the turret is circular as the turret bustle does not go all the way down; therefore the bustle part must be cut away leaving, in effect, a washer, a bustle part and the turret roof. Note also that the turret roof slopes about a quarter of the way into the bustle. Scribe the roof at this join and gently bend the part down to the relevant angle. Space the bustle part from the top with two pieces of 30 thou. and allow this assembly to dry out.

The turret sides are made from 10 thou. Cut a strip the full height of the bustle, a good deal longer than is strictly necessary. Offer it up to the rear of the turret structure and mark the places where it must be curved tightly to fit. To put the curve into the part simply make a 'U'

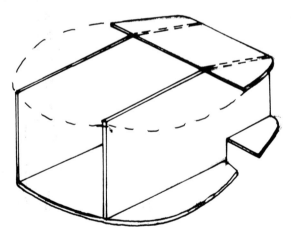

Construction of the turret: add the sides from curved 10 thou. sheet. Make up the mantlet from 20 thou. sides and a 10 thou. front; remove the shaded area when the assembly has set.

bend around a piece of small-diameter rod as shown on p. 114. Cement it in position and trim to fit. You will have to hold it for a while until the cement is set. Now cut another strip of 10 thou. to the full height of the turret, pull it under a ruler a few times until it assumes quite a tight curve and cement it to the turret top as before. Trim it to length then insert the turret-base washer. Reinforce the sides with small pieces of 10 thou. and finally fit the lower rear part of the turret from a strip of 10 thou. Again allow this unit to dry out thoroughly.

The mantlet should be tackled next. Cut a strip of 20 thou. the relevant width and bind it around a rod of the correct diameter; the handle of an Exacto craft knife is perfect in this respect. Plunge the part into hot water, leave for a few seconds then rinse well under the cold tap. The part will now be set in the curvature required. Cut out the aperture *carefully* as always, then back it with a 'plate' of 10 thou., curved in the same way. Fit the ends from 20 thou. and when it has thoroughly dried out, cut the top and bottom parts of the mantlet until they snugly match the curvature of the front of the turret. Fit the part to the turret and drill it to take the gun tube.

At first there seemed to be an easy way of reproducing the suspension. A Polish kit of their pre-war derivative of the Vickers six-tonner, the 7TP, is widely available in the United Kingdom. It is a fine model and, as it and the T26 shared a common ancestor, it might seem possible to use its suspension. However, although the parts look to be the same and are of similar dimensions there are subtle differences. In all honesty these would probably not be noticed but for my own model I decided to build the suspension from scratch.

THE WHEELS

The wheels present the first problem as, quite simply, none of the right pattern are available

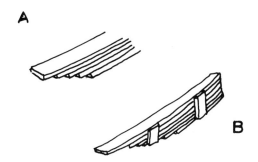

Make up springs (A) from strip-plastic detail (B).

in the correct size. However, the Airfix 1/76th scale Leopard provides wheel hubs which look right. They are too small and need tyres added to make them up to the correct diameter and thickness. To add these, cut a few long strips of 40 thou. each 3 mm (1/10th in.) wide and rub off the 'burrs' raised by cutting. Pull these strips under a ruler to curve them and then bind them, in a spiral, around a rod of slightly less diameter than the wheels. A light Exacto craft knife is exactly the correct diameter. Make sure that the strips are bound down good and tight. Fill a mug with boiling water and plunge the whole lot into it and leave for a few seconds. Lift the assembly out of the water and run under a cold tap for about thirty seconds, dry off the plastic and remove the bindings.

The result will be several tight spirals of plastic strip. Cut them into 'tyres', making sure each one is very slightly too long, then simply twist each one until it is flat. Fit them round the Airfix wheels, trim them to length and cement firmly. It is possible to develop this method to the scratch building of the wheels

The T26 from the side. Crude lettering seems to have been a feature of some Russian tanks, but it is as well not to overdo it. Note how the weathering brings out the line of the model.

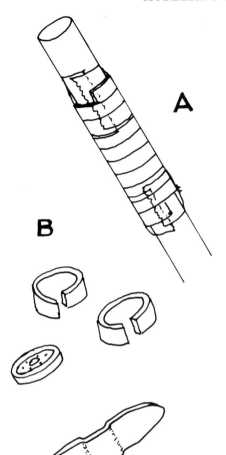

Bind a strip of plastic sheet round a rod, plunge into boiling water, then run under cold water to cool (A). Cut into tyres (B), then fit to small road wheels (from 1/76th-scale kits) to make wheels of the required size.

using a scribed-out disc of sheet as the basis and building it up to the correct section using washers of sheet, again scribed out. You need build only one pattern to act as the master for a latex mould. A latex solution can be bought from any good craft shop and is simplicity itself to use.

Join up the wheels together into twin, four-wheel units, making sure that the best wheels are on the outside where they will be seen. Note the configuration of the bogie unit: the outer bogie needs to be *decorated* with filler to produce the exact form of this part, which is slightly U-shaped as opposed to plain. (See plan.) It is a simple matter to add the central raised area from scraps of 20 thou.

Make up the springs, prototype fashion, from Microstrip or similar material.

THE SUSPENSION

The suspension arms are heat-formed from 40 thou. sheet. Carve a master pattern from balsa on fine-grained pine. Study the drawings carefully to make sure that you get it correct. It is best to start with a piece of the correct height by the length by the width. Carefully carve the shape and sand smooth. The part should be very slightly under size to allow for the

CUT BOGIE ARM FROM 20 THOU SHEET AND SIMPLY BEND TO SHAPE.

FINISH OFF TO FINAL FORM WITH MODELLING PUTTY (SHOWN SHADED) SHAPED WITH A WET KNIFE.

SMALL SCALE WHEEL SHOWN WITH TYRE FITTED TO ACHIEVE THE CORRECT SIZE.

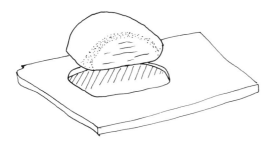

Carve a master from wood and sand smooth; make the female from thick cardboard.

Make sure the master passes easily through the female.

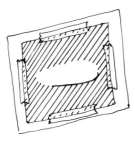

Tape plastic sheet to the female. Hold up to light to see through the plastic card and draw round the aperture.

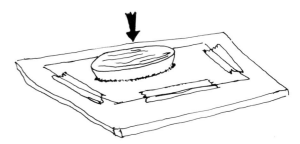

Place the assembly under a heat source, such as a grill. When the plastic sheet begins to smoke, blacken and go floppy, remove it from the heat and plunge the master through the card as indicated by the drawn shape.

Allow to cool and remove the formed plastic card.

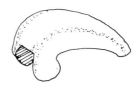

Trim to shape.

thickness of the plastic, which is formed over this the 'male' mould. Draw, on a square of thick cardboard, around the base of the pattern and then cut out the shape to leave a hole through which the pattern can easily pass with rather under a millimetre to spare all round. Tape a good-sized piece of sheet over the hole and hold it up to the light. You should be able

to see the shape of the hole through the sheet, so mark it in with a pencil. Heat this assembly, sheet side uppermost, under a grill on a low setting. When the sheet begins to smoke and go floppy, plunge the pattern through the aperture using the pencil mark as a guide. It is actually a lot easier done than said and, as always, a little practice makes perfect. Allow the formed sheet to cool, remove it from the cardboard and cut the suspension arm out. Repeat the process four times (at least) to make up four identical suspension arms.

Make up the suspension units as shown on p. 115. They are quite delicate so go easy on the cement and then allow them to set. When you are sure they are set and strong, drill the inside of the suspension arm to accept a supporting rod of plastic tube, then drill the lower hull to accept these four units. Cement them in place and allow to set.

After this everything else is easy or at least it seems that way.

FINISHING

Make the final drive housing from 80 thou. sanded to shape. The drive sprockets and idlers are made in similar fashion. Begin by scribing washers of 20 thou. Mark in the position of the teeth as shown opposite/above and carefully remove the unwanted parts with a knife fitted with a new, very sharp blade. Cut the inner spokes from a disc of the same material and fit and decorate as necessary. The idlers need tyres made from 10 thou. sheet.

It is not necessary to explain exactly how the rest of the model is made up. Once the three main parts, the hull, the turret and the suspension, are conquered the rest is very basic modelling. When the main parts are fabricated it is a very good idea to make up a checklist of the remaining work. As each piece is completed, it should be crossed off.

The tracks for my model came from an Italeri M13/40 which had been savaged by a very small dog! Fortunately the tracks were not damaged and they look about right and are a very good fit. Had these not been available the tracks themselves could have been made up ladder-fashion as shown opposite/below. This is a tedious task and you may think it worthwhile to buy a kit just for the tracks.

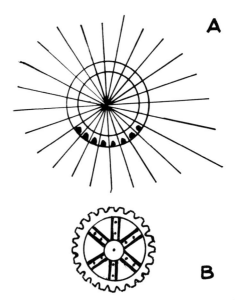

Mark out the drive sprocket as shown in A and remove shaded areas. B shows the finished item. Make up the idlers in the same manner.

Finishing off and presenting a model like this is largely a matter of personal choice. This model certainly deserves a crew but too much stowage may hide painstakingly executed handiwork. Fortunately, Russian vehicles of

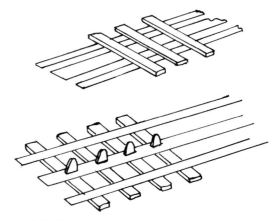

Scratch build tracks ladder-fashion as shown.

this period were fairly bare of personal effects, which probably reflected the state of Russian society at the time. Extensive weathering does, however, bring out the detail and shape of this vehicle most effectively and adds a certain degree of authenticity.

Once you have successfully tackled a model of this degree of difficulty future projects will hold few terrors for you. Obviously projects will appeal to the individual which are much more difficult, involved, unresearched and time-consuming but once the basics are known and can be confidently put into practice, they can be adapted to any model at all.

Further Reading

Out-of-print publications

Much early material is now no longer available including many sources which were considered standard when the hobby became popular. The following are well worth purchasing if they can be found second-hand.

Airfix Publications – Patrick Stephens
They offered a brief series of books keyed to models manufactured by Airfix.

Almark Publications
This company published a series of small-format books on military subjects during the 1960s through to the early 1970s. Generally regarded as ideal introductions to their subject. The quality varied but anything illustrated by Kenneth M. Jones, the present editor of *Military Modelling* magazine, is well worth buying.

Bellona Prints – Argus Specialist publications
The series which started most modellers off. Splendid 1/76th scale drawings of military vehicles. The early issues consisted of four-view plans, a brief history of the vehicle and a photograph. Four vehicles were covered in these issues. Later series covered a single vehicle type in more detail and also provided drawings in 1/48th scale. These publications are very much sought-after.

Profile publications
Each profile covered the development and history of a specific vehicle in some depth. Good photographic coverage and artwork which, although sometimes suspect, could act as the basis of a model.

Current publications

MAGAZINES

Airfix magazine – Alan W. Hall
This famous name is again available and usually features articles and reviews of interest.

Military Modelling – Argus Specialist publications
Still the best magazine on the market which features first class AFV articles every issue. Ken Jones, the editor is himself a fine modeller and one of the best vehicle illustrators and historians there is.

Military Hobbies – A.E. Morgan publications
This magazine, a very good mix of model soldier and model armoured vehicle features, has been going for a couple of years now and is published twice-monthly. It is particularly recommended for basic features and reviews. The quality of this magazine is steadily improving and it is becoming more and more AFV oriented.

BOOK SERIES

Vanguard – Osprey Publishing
A comprehensive series describing vehicles and famous military units of the twentieth century. Very well written and illustrated with good photographs and fine artwork.

Tanks Illustrated – Arms and Armour Press
Extensive photographic coverage of specific vehicles. Excellent captions. They provide

modellers with the sort of material needed to bring models to life.

Squadron – Signal Publications
These are the natural successors to Bellona Prints. They have evolved to give very comprehensive coverage of famous specific vehicles. Historical coverage is excellent and very well supported by photographs, fine scale drawings and spectacular colour artwork. Exactly tailored to modellers' needs and highly recommended.

World War II Photo Albums – Patrick Stephens
Useful photographic coverage from German Archive sources, the same applies to this series as to *Tanks Illustrated*.

The best society for AFV modellers is the Miniature Armoured Fighting Vehicles Association (MAFVA). It produces an excellent magazine worth the subscription charge alone. Write to: Gary Williams, 15 Berwick Avenue, Heaton Mersey, Stockport, Cheshire, SK4 3AA.

Afterword

Between the writing of this book and publication the manufacturers seem to have realized that there is a resurgence of interest in the hobby and have responded accordingly. Much of this interest has been aroused by the smaller manufacturers, the so-called 'cottage industry', who have now gained a very high profile within the hobby.

Tamiya have released a splendid late model 'Tiger' which makes their elderly 'early' model look decidedly dated. They are also due to release a Russian IS2 heavy tank, and the word on the grapevine is that it is one of their best models ever. At the time of writing the first of their series of late type Sd Kfz 251s, the German armoured half track troop carrier, is being prepared for release.

The American firm Lindberg have released a Russian T55, a vehicle still in widespread service, in 1/35th scale, but I am decidedly disappointed – it appears to be both inaccurate and poorly detailed.

Dragon are a new concern (to me) and have their base in the Far East. Their first two models are of the current Russian BMP 1&2 infantry fighting vehicles. They are very nice kits and the future releases augur well judging from this standard; but it is noticeable that both models are not quite as accurate as most current ones.

Esci have released quite a large range of modern Russian and American equipment, the tracked vehicles having 'link and length' tracks, which are frankly the kits' best features. The detailing looks somewhat half-hearted, but they are capable of being worked up to a very high standard.

Italeri continue to get maximum mileage out of their Shermans' chassis, but whilst the new bits are quite nice the tracks and running gear need quite radical revision – not because the parts are poorly moulded, but rather that these patterns of running gear were not used on the new variants. Their saving grace is that they are quite cheap.

Verlinden products have released a new series of vehicles, largely current Russian items, under the Trophy label. Impeccably cast, as usual, they are not quite as accurate as I would have expected, are solid so that they cannot be 'opened up' and the undersides are decidedly 'semi scale'. It's as well that these parts are not normally visible. My own feeling is that this concern is largely trading upon its reputation!

Gunze Sangyo have brought out a most unusual vehicle: the 10.5 cm leFH PanzerFeld-Haurbitze GW 39 H (f). It consists of the excellent Heller chassis and lots of the parent company's hi-tech bits in etched brass, metal and plastic. There are also a set of Model Kastern tracks enclosed. Very highly detailed, very nearly right and very expensive.

Sovereign miniatures have released a new German Bergpanther recovery vehicle, a Humber armoured car and another Ferret. They are all very pleasant models but not quite up to the highest standards. Attractively priced, though, for resin-cast products.

Accurate Armour goes from strength to strength with a lot of new releases of the highest quality. The first of their proposed series of 'super heavy' tanks, the German E100, is now available and is a superb piece of model-making. New accessory parts include turrets, tracks and figures.

Cromwell models also continue to amaze me. A few years ago I would not have believed that they could improve upon their standards in 1/76th scale, but they have, and are by far the best small-scale models available. They have also moved up into 1/35th scale with most impressive results. Their first two sets of larger-scale crew figures are equally good.

MB models, of the United States, have introduced a series of Sherman accessory hulls, turrets and sets of running gear etc. They are all impressively accurate.

Led Sled have brought out a very good 1/35th scale Bofors light AA gun.

Al-By have moved into the injection-moulded side of things with a very neat and accurate Panhard armoured car of Second World War vintage. This has allowed them to reach a rather wider market.

These are only the products which have caught my eye. There are many others, all – or nearly all – of the highest quality. Things are looking pretty good for the military vehicle modeller.

Index